Contemporary Fashion Dolls
The Next Generation

by Beth Owens

This special edition *Tyler Wentworth*, limited to 500 pieces, was created for the 2000 Santa Fe Doll Art event. *Photo courtesy of the Robert Tonner Doll Company.*

Hobby House Press, Inc.
Grantsville, MD 21536
www.hobbyhouse.com

Acknowledgments

I wish to thank the following for their assistance and support in the writing of this book:

My husband David, my sons Charles and Andrew, and my parents, Leon and Odonna DeRock.

Mel Odom, Joan Greene, Linda Masterson, Beth Maxwell, Frank Rotundo and Vince Nowell of Ashton-Drake's *Gene* team.

Robert Tonner and Nancy Shomo at the Robert Tonner Doll Company.

Michelle Dooley at The Franklin Mint.

Gale Jarvis, Herb Brown, Deb Dillingham and Steve Skutka at the Alexander Doll Company and Willie Norkin and Julie Nurenberg at Sally Fischer Public Relations.

Gretchen McGinnis of L. L. Knickerbocker and Bryan Ventura.

Jennifer Klausner and Jill Nordquist at Mattel.

Margiann Flanagan at Effanbee and Renée Turcott of the Zachary Group.

Norman Libman at Kingstate and Holly Miner.

Patricia Lewis and Morgan Mahoney of The Family Company.

Tom Wallace and Susan Wakeen of the Susan Wakeen Doll Company.

A. Glenn Mandeville, Adele Stitsworth, Marlene Mura, Karen Caviale, Sonia Rivera, Nick Hill, Barbara "Bopsy" Blazer, Cindy Kent, Suzanne Bowns, Deb Lustman, Teri Gallagher, Dianne Carson, Jana Cornell, Phyllis Evanson, Rebecca Brosdahl, Jane Brooks, Susan Howard, Mary Soranno, Tom Courtney, Judy Harbaugh, Linda Braun, Randy Wilson, Sherry Miller, Doris Mixon, Mary DeWitt, Aurea Vilar, Judy LaManna, Anne-Marie Burns, Susan Manos, Mary Beyer, Debra Aguila-Weinstein, Marie Raymond, Jay Searle, Robin Pricer, Lynda M. Phillips, Kathryn Rose, Helen Golden, Susan Moe, Jim Faraone, Jerry Parzer, Lloyd Baker and Travis Manning for practical help and emotional support as I needed it.

I wish to thank Dan and Barbara Miller for giving me a start in my writing career and for their years of support.

The staff at Hobby House Press, including Gary Ruddell, Brenda Wiseman, Jennifer Hare, Theresa Black, Brenda Ruggerio and anyone else associated with this project. Also Carolyn Cook for her help and support.

And last but not least I'd like to acknowledge the contributions of two very special people, Doug James and Laura Meisner. Without them, I doubt that this project would have ever even been conceived. Doug and Laura took pictures, let me pick their brains, provided information and insight and have been more than generous with their time. Together and individually, they have been a tremendous source of support and inspiration. I am honored that they are my friends.

Front Cover Center: *Party of the Season Tyler Wentworth* from 1999. *Photo courtesy of the Robert Tonner Doll Company.*
Upper Right & Clockwise: *Iced Coffee Gene* from 1997, *photo courtesy of Ashton-Drake; James Purcell Cissy* from 1999, *photo courtesy of Sally Fischer Public Relations and the Alexander Doll Company; Rose DeWitt Butaker,* the heroine of the movie Titanic, *photo courtesy of The Franklin Mint;* and *Anniversary Gala Brenda Starr* from the 2000 line, *photo courtesy of Effanbee and The Zachary Group.* **Back Cover:** Prototype *Willow in Autumn Colors* and prototype *Daisy in Trafalgar Square,* two of the dressed dolls in the Somers & Field line for 1999. *Photo courtesy of L. L. Knickerbocker.*

Contemporary Fashion Dolls: The Next Generation is an independent study by the author Beth Owens and published by Hobby House Press, Inc. The research and publication of this book was not sponsored in any way by the manufacturers of the doll, the doll costumes and the doll accessories featured in this study. Photographs of the collectibles were from dolls, costumes or accessories belonging to the author, manufacturers of the dolls or others credited within the caption.

Additional copies of this book may be purchased at $24.95 (plus postage and handling) from
Hobby House Press, Inc.
1 Corporate Drive, Grantsville, MD 21536
1-800-554-1447
www.hobbyhouse.com
or from your favorite bookstore or dealer.
© 2000 Beth Owens

Printed in the United States of America.

ISBN: 0-87588-576-4

Table of Contents

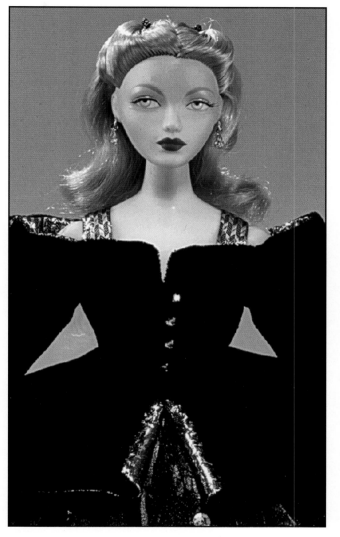

The first *Gene* to retire was *Premiere*, issued in 1995 and retired in 1997. *Photo courtesy Ashton-Drake.*

Don't miss the *Contemporary Fashion Dolls: The Next Generation* Internet update, which includes regularly updated fashion doll news and values compiled by Beth Owens. Visit the Hobby House Press web site at www.hobbyhouse.com, and click on Beth's Spotlight on Fashion Dolls.

Dedication

This book is dedicated to my family.
To my parents, Leon and Odonna DeRock,
who indulged my childhood passions for dolls and books.
To my sons, Charles and Andrew Owens, who don't seem to
mind a mother who plays with dolls.
To my husband, David Owens, who has learned to
live with a house full of little vinyl women.
I love you all!

Prototype *Willow in Autumn Colors* and prototype *Daisy in Trafalgar Square*, two of the dressed dolls in the Somers & Field line for 1999. *Photo courtesy of L. L. Knickerbocker.*

Foreword

by A. Glenn Mandeville

Today at the dawn of a new Millennium, we are entering the third "Golden Age of Fashion Dolls". From the first age of the French fashion dolls, it took almost 70 years for the next gilded moments to arrive. The dolls of the 1950s such as Madame Alexander's *Cissy*, Ideal's *Revlon* and American Character's *Sweet Sue* and *Toni* dolls reflected the desire of children to no longer play in the present, but to indulge their peacetime childhoods in pursuit of a new type of person, the teenager! The introduction of the *Barbie®* doll by Mattel in 1959 told the story of her generation and today still is one of the most popular dolls in the world with children and adults.

The third golden age of fashion dolls arrived in the guise of a fictional 16-inch 1940s movie star doll named *Gene*. Created by Mel Odom and the Ashton-Drake Galleries, she did not start out as a play doll for children, but was marketed directly to adults.

Since 1995 the fashion doll phenomena has been at the forefront of doll collecting. As we enter the next century, the choices have never been better as more and more fashion dolls in never before dreamed of sizes aimed at the adult collector vie for a place on the runway of fame and fortune. The fashion doll collector is now a recognized part of the doll world, with festivals held in Paris and soon in Chicago!

In this exciting and groundbreaking book, authority Beth Owens has woven a tale of a nation in love with being young, carefree and glamorous.

Her story is one that if you did not live as a child, a second chance is now being offered. Her blending of the familiar plus the many new choices offer the reader a never before glimpse into the past and today of a relatively new type of doll.

For adults new to the hobby, Beth has taken the reader on a pop culture journey from dolls that began life as children's toys to the haute couture fashions dolls sold for thousands that are just for the adult collector.

Beth Owens has a wonderful tradition of putting so much of her own life and experiences into her work. Here she is at her glowing best showing her readers the past, the present and what all of us fashion doll collectors feel will be the glorious future of yet another aspect of her hobby.

As a lifetime doll collector, historian, author, columnist and retailer, my life has been about fashion dolls. No one, in my opinion, has told the story of the genre better than Beth Owens. This is one book that you will want to read over and over again.

It isn't just about dolls, the book is about us. Beth has captured our dreams of what life could be like in a world filled with glamour, fashion, fame and fortune. Through our dolls, many of our dreams can come true.

With the wisdom in this book, however, your dreams just might turn into a reality. Thanks, Beth, for a wonderful walk down the runways of life....A. Glenn Mandeville

Introduction

It's been a long day and you're hungry and stressed. Breakfast was just a cup of coffee; lunch was your customary yogurt and bagel. For dinner, your family or friends suggest going out, but not to the restaurant to which you usually go. The food there is good, of course, but why not try something different? They want to go to that new buffet restaurant that just opened in your area. You're skeptical; many of these places are chaotic and frantic, little more than glorified cafeterias. And you've had a hard day and want the nice, relaxing evening you've come to expect at your usual place. But they insist, so you go anyway. Thankfully, your concerns vanish as you walk through the door. It's busy, but you're immediately put at ease with attractive, tasteful décor and a cozy atmosphere. After getting a place to sit, you wander over to the buffet table, upon which you find a most sumptuous spread. Your nose tingles as the smell of your favorite foods mingles delightfully with the aroma of new dishes you have not tried before. To your left is a beloved comfort food from your childhood and to your right is something spicy and exotic. You take a generous helping of one dish and a more modest sampling of another. Some of the new things you try you love but there are others that, while tasty, just don't suit your palate. But that's okay. There are no rules that say you have to love every dish on the buffet. Because you're so hungry and the food is so good, you go back for seconds. You get more of the foods you liked the best, skip the things that didn't appeal to you and hope you have room for some of the delectable desserts.

The hobby of collecting contemporary fashion dolls is much like the aforementioned experience of dining at a wonderful, sumptuous buffet. (Without the calories, of course!) For years, enthusiasts interested in collecting current fashion dolls were limited pretty much to *Barbie®* dolls. In essence,

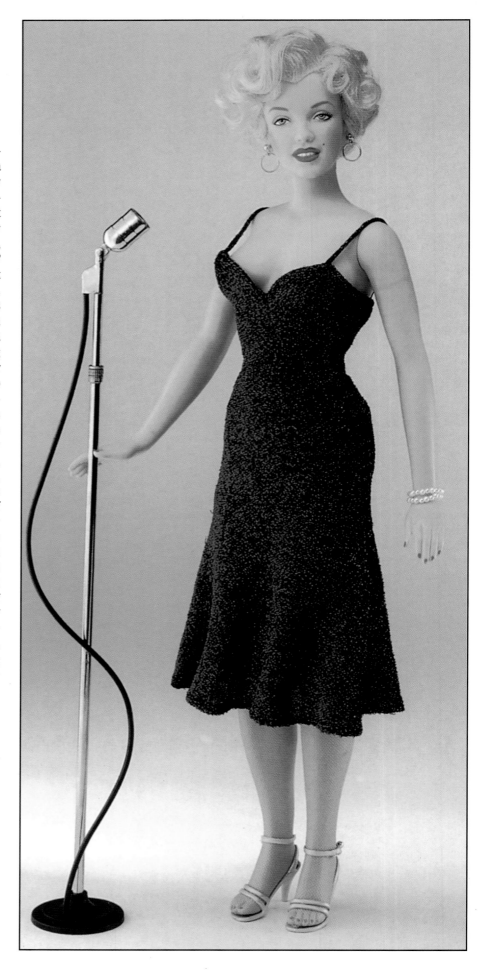

Platinum *Simply Gene. Photo courtesy of Ashton-Drake.*

Opposite Page: *Marilyn Monroe* was also translated breathtakingly into fashion doll form by The Franklin Mint. Here she appears as she was entertaining the troops during the Korean War. *Photo courtesy of The Franklin Mint.*

Barbie® dolls were everyone's "favorite dish", and the multitudinous array of different interpretations of *Barbie*® dolls satisfied our collective appetites…for a while. However, the hobby evolved from a one-course meal to a veritable buffet with the phenomenal success of *Gene* and the subsequent introduction of other large fashion dolls marketed specifically to adult collectors. Just as *Barbie*® dolls set the standard for fashion dolls meant for children, *Gene* set a new standard for fashion dolls meant for adults. Indeed, *Gene* has spawned an entire new generation of collectible fashion dolls.

While the perimeters for the new genre of collectible fashion dolls are flexible, there are several definitive characteristics. First is size; most of these dolls are 15 to 16 inches tall, but several are even larger. Second is the notion that these are essentially play dolls for adults. These dolls are intended to be removed from the box and handled. Unlike the previous generation of collectible fashion dolls, they do not lose value if they are taken out of the box to be displayed, as long as they are kept in original condition. Furthermore, they are durable, made of vinyl or hard plastic. Porcelain is too fragile and intimidating a medium for the fashion doll enthusiast and discourages interactivity. Fashion doll collectors, regardless of age, want to play! Third, these dolls are made primarily for adults, catering to mature tastes and sensibilities. Their story lines are often sophisticated and complex, centering on irresistible fantasies such as being a movie star in the glamorous 1940s or being the hottest young designer on Seventh Avenue today. The dolls' ensembles, whether meticulously accurate for the time or merely suggestive of a certain period, are often made of fine fabrics such as silk, wool and linen. Last, these dolls represent adults or teenagers, not children. Most female fashion dolls have permanently arched feet to accommodate high heels and sport realistic, womanly bodies, some with anatomically correct breasts. While this might seem shocking and inappropriate to some in a doll meant for children, keep in mind that the target audience for these dolls is adult collectors.

Just as every dish lends its own unique flavor to a meal, each doll contributes something unique and special to this new genre of fashion dolls. *Gene* embodies the glamour of 1940s and '50s Hollywood, cheerful musicals and romantic comedies as well as film *noir.* Depending on her clothes and hair, *Gene* can convey the essence of nearly every famous actress during that time, from Ginger Rogers to Rita Hayworth to Marilyn Monroe. Madame Alexander's revamped *Cissy* is the result of a marriage of fantasy and high fashion with a dollop of extravagance and opulence that takes her over the top but not over the edge. Robert Tonner's *American Models* have an essence of understated elegance and a quiet, timeless air. *Tyler Wentworth* is imbued with a similar sense of classic, contemporary chic but with a trendy touch. *The Mod British Birds, Willow Somers* and *Daisy Field,* bring an upscale sensibility to the Age of Aquarius, with the exuberant styles and psychedelic colors that typified "Youthquake" of the late '60s and early '70s. Additionally, *Daisy* is particularly significant in that she is the first ethnic main character in a line. The fashion dolls of The Franklin Mint pay homage to heroines real and fictional. Among their offerings are vinyl dolls that depict First Lady *Jackie Kennedy, Princess Diana, Marilyn Monroe, Scarlett O'Hara* and *Titanic's Rose DeWitt Bukater.* And of course these are just the dolls that were available at the end of 1999. *Eve, Alex, Micki* and *Kitty Collier* are a few of the new names on collectors' lips in 2000. Who knows how many more dolls there will eventually be in this genre?

But wait a minute! What about the *Barbie*® doll? Isn't she a contemporary fashion doll? Isn't she included in this book? The answer is yes…and no. The *Barbie*® doll is the most influential fashion doll of all time. It is unlikely that any of these new fashion dolls, with the possible exception of the '90s version of *Cissy,* would even exist had *Barbie*® dolls never been created. Thus, we will look at the *Barbie*® doll from a historical standpoint and examine how she defined the previous genre of fashion dolls meant for children's play and how the hobby of *Barbie*® doll collecting inspired the creation of today's adult collectible fashion dolls. However, this book does not focus on *Barbie*® dolls and similar dolls, such as Hamilton Design's *Candi,* in the same way that it concentrates on the dolls that comprise this new generation. While 11-½-inch dolls are wonderful, very collectible and have large, enthusiastic followings, they truly deserve their own classification and are a genre unto themselves. To get back to the food analogy, it's as if we'd lumped a recipe for wild rice casserole into a cookbook of pasta salads because, well, they're all starches, right? Wrong. Moreover, there are many excellent *Barbie*® doll books already available, several of which are listed among the references for this book.

This hobby is like a sumptuous feast, and it is ours to enjoy. I hope you will enjoy this look at the next generation of contemporary fashion dolls, and, please, come back for seconds!

*1999 Holiday Cissy.
Photo courtesy of
Sally Fischer Public
Relations and the
Alexander Doll
Company.*

Confessions of a Fashion Doll Collector

As is the case with many collectors, my love of fashion dolls began with my childhood *Barbie®* dolls. An only child, I spent many hours engrossed in imaginative play with *Barbie®* dolls, *Francie, Skipper* and *Skooter*. My *Twist 'N Turn Barbie®* was particularly well-loved; her hip was sprung from riding *Jane West's* horse, her hair was cut into what I thought was a stylish do, and her face was smeared with ink after I used a ball point pen to enhance her eye makeup. It was with mixed emotions that I eventually replaced her with a shiny new *Living Barbie®*. I was thrilled to have such a gorgeous, perfect doll and yet, because I was getting to the age at which most girls put away their dolls, I felt profoundly sad. This was the last *Barbie®* doll I would ever buy for myself.

Or so I thought!

Years later, when I was expecting my first child, I often wandered through the doll aisles of toy and discount stores when I was shopping for things the baby would need. I looked at the baby dolls, the *Cabbage Patch Kids* and, of course, the *Barbie®* dolls. Seeing the new incarnations of *Barbie®* dolls brought back fond memories of my girlhood and I happily anticipated the fun my "daughter" would eventually have with her *Barbie®* dolls. Maybe the two of us could start collecting *Barbie®* dolls; it sounded like such a fun hobby to share with a little girl.

However, my first child turned out to be a boy, as did my second! I resigned myself to a lifetime of *Legos*, cars and action figures and figured the only way I'd have dolls in my life was to buy them for other people's children. It hadn't occurred to me that doll collecting was something I could do by and for myself.

When my boys were a little older, I felt an acute need for something special just for me. A stay-at-home mom, I was starting to feel like I was losing myself in a world that revolved around potty training and *Sesame Street*. I yearned for something that could be a respite from the demands of everyday life as well as an enjoyable creative outlet. I'd tried crafts, but there are only so many hand-painted sweatshirts that one person can wear. Why not collect something? I thought about *Barbie®* dolls, but by then my girlhood companions were gone, the inelegant victims of a flooded basement. I assumed that no other doll could ever be as special to me as the ones from my childhood, so why bother trying to replace them? However, I still had my beloved childhood trolls, so I began collecting them instead.

One-of-a-kind *USO Gene* created by designer Doug James, auctioned at the first *Gene* convention in 1996.
Photo courtesy of J. Douglas James.

Opposite Page: Susan Wakeen's *Eve* is a new entry on the fashion doll scene in 2000. *Photo courtesy of the Susan Wakeen Doll Company.*

It was 1992 and trolls were the hot collector craze at that time. I had a blast searching gift shops and candy stores to find new ones and eventually I discovered vintage trolls in antique stores and at flea markets. Wanting to learn as much as I could about trolls, I started scouring the collectibles section of the local bookstores, trying to find as many references as possible. At that time, there were no books devoted to trolls, so I began perusing general doll books and magazines, hoping to unearth some sort of information. One day, I spotted an issue of *Barbie® Bazaar* at the local bookstore. I couldn't believe it: a magazine, aimed at adults, devoted to *Barbie®* doll collecting! It was a stunning revelation to thumb through that first issue and realize that *Barbie®* doll collecting was indeed a legitimate hobby for adults. It was okay to enjoy *Barbie®* dolls as an adult, and, while it would have been enjoyable to share the hobby with a child, it was something I could do alone. As I bought more books and amassed back issues of *Barbie® Bazaar*, I felt an excitement and enthusiasm that had been missing from my everyday routine. This was the something special I needed. My fate was sealed and *Barbie®* dolls were back in my life.

Well, sort of. I was utterly charmed by the *Barbie®* doll's friend *Midge*, a doll that I didn't own as a child. At the first doll show I ever attended, I bought several collectibles, including a rather mousy, nondescript brunette *Midge* with rubbed lips, and to my surprise, she very deeply touched my heart. The other dolls I bought were beautiful, but somehow they weren't special like that little *Midge*. I studied the reference books and the old issues of *Barbie® Bazaar* and was amazed to see the many variations of vintage *Midge*. By the time I attended my next show, barely a month after the first one, I had decided to focus my collection on amassing those variations as well as obtaining all the contemporary *Midge* dolls. Before long, I learned how to reroot and repaint and I began to customize *Midge* to my liking, just as I had done with my beloved *Twist 'N Turn*, only this time I actually knew what I was doing![1] As the array of collector edition *Barbie®* dolls expanded, I didn't want to be left out of the fun, even though my heart was with *Midge*. So I bought many of those collector dolls, from store specials to *Classiques*, and redressed customized *Midge* dolls in the outfits. I knew I was "devaluing" those collectibles, but it didn't matter. I was having fun.

My single-minded passion for *Midge* continued unabated for the next several years until I was hit with a double whammy. First, I completed my collection. There were a few rarities that I was missing and I was always eager to buy whatever new *Midge* dolls Mattel put on the market. But for the most part, I was satisfied with what I had.

What next? Second, the hobby was gripped in a state of chaos and turmoil at that particular time. I began collecting just before the *Barbie®* doll frenzy caught fire and I watched something that had been an enjoyable pastime for enthusiasts who loved the doll turn into a craze that spun rapidly out of control. Those maddeningly intense years of the mid '90s took a major toll on the spirits of many collectors, including mine. We all watched in horror as speculators and scalpers, people who cared not for *Barbie®* dolls but for the profit they promised, hoarded as many special editions as they could and created an astronomical, artificial demand for more. As Mattel responded with not only higher production numbers but also an ever-increasing multitude of new collector series and editions, we felt overwhelmed. We couldn't keep up, whether we really wanted to or not. Additionally, the great box debate divided the hobby, with some collectors defiantly insisting that dolls be removed from their boxes in order to be enjoyed and others equally adamant about keeping them NRFB (Never Removed From the Box). As time went on, the general mood of the hobby turned to frustration and malaise. Some quit altogether and other die-hard *Barbie®* doll enthusiasts began exploring other fashion dolls. Indeed, it was almost like a dark little secret when *Barbie®* doll collectors would discreetly confess to each other, "I collect *Gene*."

To be sure, I had taken notice of Ashton-Drake's *Gene Marshall* when she was introduced. Ever since I was a teenager, I had been fascinated with the popular culture of the 1940s, the music and the movies and especially the clothes, and here was this new fashion doll that epitomized all of that. So did I start buying *Gene* that first year? Of course not! I knew what I loved and I wasn't about to try something different. I was a focused, dedicated *Barbie®* doll, no, *Midge* collector and I wasn't going to get into any other dolls. Besides, *Gene* was huge! If I collected *Gene*, I'd have to reconfigure the shelving in my doll room and find new ways to display my dolls. Around that same time, a couple of other fashion dolls briefly piqued my interest, but good grief! Those Tonner *American Models* and Alexander's upscale, updated *Cissy* were even bigger than *Gene*! I didn't have room in my life for such huge dolls!

And then came the two *Gene* dolls that melted my heart. Among the 1997 *Gene* introductions was the doll I simply could not resist. *Iced Coffee's,* simple but complex design, rich yet subtle colors and gorgeous red hair pulled into a snood made me succumb to the charms of the lovely *Miss Marshall*. To me, she was everything attractive and elegant about the 1940s, and even

---

1 Any changes to the doll that cannot be completely reversed will not be as desirable to collectors and therefore its value may be adversely affected.

Above: Three *Dam Trolls* from mid-1960s. *Author's childhood collection.*

Above Right: Rerooted *Twist 'N Turn Reproduction Barbie®* doll in vintage Mattel fashion, *Flower Wower*, my favorite outfit from childhood.

Right: This lovely 1964 *Midge* has a charmingly sweet face sprinkled with freckles and blue eyes that glance slightly to her left. It's no wonder *Midge* ruled my heart and my collection for so long! She is dressed in *Campus Sweetheart*.

though I still had reservations about her size, I ordered her anyway. The other *Gene* that spoke to my heart was a one-of-a-kind *USO* created for the first *Gene* convention. Although I had no military experience, as a former registered nurse I had a deep fascination with the heroism and bravery of women in uniform during World War II: the nurses, the WACs, even the entertainers who visited the troops. The notion of a fashion doll dressed in uniform to represent these women was a cherished fantasy I had held for some time, and to see it embodied so perfectly and succinctly in that one-of-a-kind *Gene* hit me right in the heart. Okay, so it wasn't love at first sight, but maybe collecting *Gene* wasn't such a terrible idea after all.

Because *Iced Coffee* wasn't to be released until later that year and *USO* was, at that time, not even in production, I ordered a *Blue Goddess* and a *Pin-Up* right away. But I didn't have much of a chance to enjoy them because we were moving to a new community, to a house with thankfully a larger room for my dolls. My interest in dolls had to be sidelined for awhile and my brand-new *Gene* dolls were packed away with my *Midge* collection. So much for a great beginning!

Red Venus Gene, restyled hair, in *Striking Gold*. Both from 1995, manufactured by Ashton-Drake Galleries. She is also wearing a mink stole from *House of Harcat*.

However, another *Gene* came to the rescue and sealed my fate. On the day we moved into our new house, I found a little yellow slip from one of the delivery services on the door. To my chagrin, on the deck in back were two rain-soaked boxes marked "Ashton-Drake." Even though I really didn't have time, I opened the packages right away because I was worried sick that the doll and her extra outfit had been ruined. Luckily, *Red Venus* was only slightly soggy and *Striking Gold* was still dry. I quickly redressed *Gene* because I was worried that the damp dress might stain her body and placed her on a moving box in our living room.

As silly as it may sound, having that one *Gene* on that extremely stressful moving day somehow made it seem a little less trying. And somehow, having her on display made the new house seem more like home. Little by little, more *Genes* came to live at our new home, and in redressing them or simply combing their hair I experienced the same enjoyment and sense of respite that I always had felt with my *Midge* collection.

Once I had diversified, there was no turning back. As my interest and affection for *Gene* grew, I backtracked to get the outfits and dolls I had missed by not buying her in the beginning. And then I succumbed to the charms of Madame

Alexander's dolls. I had recently visited a doll shop and saw in person the adorable 1997 *Coco*. I didn't buy *Coco* because I decided she was too expensive and just too different for my taste – and then I obsessed about her for a week and had to go back to the shop to get her. What a wonderful doll she was! She had three outfits, a ton of accessories and even a fuzzy, dust-mop beanbag dog. How could I resist? Of course, once I was smitten with *Coco*, there was no reason not to start buying *Cissy*. Somehow *Cissy* just didn't seem so gargantuan anymore and I slid down a slippery slope into a new passion. Later in the year I became enchanted with the beautiful face of *Julia*, the doll created by Robert Tonner for the Georgetown Collection. This made me look more seriously at the beautiful *American Models* by the Robert Tonner Doll Co. and another facet was added to my collection. And how could I resist the Tonner Company's newest superstar, *Tyler Wentworth*? At Toy Fair 1999, I literally stopped dead in my tracks at the L. L. Knickerbocker display of the prototype *Somers & Field* dolls. I admired the *Gene* designs of the doll's creators, Laura Meisner and Doug James (who, respectively, designed *Iced Coffee* and *USO*) and their new creative collaboration was fabulous. I simply had to have these groovy dolls and their fashions in my life. And let's not forget Effanbee's *Brenda Starr*, a doll whose reincarnation I had been hoping for since I had discovered Madame Alexander's 1960s interpretation. And Franklin Mint's *Titanic* Rose? I loved that movie and Kate Winslet, and I had to have that doll, too. (You know, I still buy *Barbie®* dolls…and *Midge*…and I collect Takara's *Jenny*, too. Do you think my husband would mind if we moved again, maybe to a bigger house?)

Seriously, I used to think that the only way to collect was to focus all of one's passion and enthusiasm quite narrowly: to stick to only the doll one loved the most and forsake any others. For some people, that is exactly the way they should collect; if they're happier by limiting the scope of their collections, that's wonderful. In my case, however, I changed and, as a result, my collection had to change as well. No, I don't feel the exact same passion toward each and every doll. Of course I have my favorites; some dolls simply appeal to me more than others do and I'd be hard-pressed to part with them if I had to thin out my collection. Some days I find I want to concentrate on one sort of doll, on other days, another. However, I truly find all of them special. Each individual doll adds something distinctive and unique to my collection. Just as with people, the whole is far more interesting than merely the sum of the parts. I am glad that I collect fashion dolls and that I opened my heart to new experiences. It's been an interesting adventure, and one that is far from complete.

Madeline from the *American Models Collection*, made in 1998 by the Robert Tonner Doll Company.

Secrets Cissy, made in 1997 by the Alexander Doll Company, relaxes in one of her lingerie ensembles. *Ty Beanie Baby* cat, butterfly hair clip, book and custom chaise lounge added by author.

The *Mod British Birds* made many collectors stand up and take notice of the wonderful upscale possibilities of the Mod era. The prototypes of *Daisy in Trafalgar Square* (opposite page) and *Willow in Autumn Colors* (this page) literally stopped this author in her tracks at Toy Fair 1999.

Above: *Cissy* mid- to late 1950s. Alexander Doll Company. *From the collection of Laura Meisner, photo by James & Meisner.*

Right: 18-inch French Fashion Doll, possibly Jumeau. *From the collection of Laura Meisner photo by James & Meisner.*

Chapter One

The History of Contemporary Fashion Dolls

The story of contemporary fashion dolls actually begins in the mid 19th century, when exquisite, French-made lady dolls were at the height of their popularity. Also known as Parisiennes or *poupées modèles*, French fashion dolls were originally intended to serve as three-dimensional models of the style of the day for upper class women and their dressmakers. When they were rendered obsolete for this purpose by the proliferation of fashion magazines and fashion plates, the dolls retained their popularity, becoming playthings for wealthy girls and intimate gifts for affluent young ladies. An entire industry rose up around French fashion dolls in the latter half of the 1800s. The dolls required stylish clothing, often commissioned from the finest fashion designers such as the House of Worth. They had numerous accessories from hats, gloves and shoes to jewelry and parasols to furniture and even miniature fashion dolls of their own. At least two magazines regularly published patterns so girls and their mothers could create costumes for the dolls at home. And at least one shop, *Au Paradis des Enfants* in Paris, distributed a tiny catalog of dolls and fashions to its customers.

However, interest in French fashion dolls began to wane in the 1880s. Changes in cultural attitudes toward children and the emergence of a middle class increased demand for affordable play dolls. To meet this demand, bébés and other childlike dolls that better resembled their potential owners were introduced, and fashionable lady dolls fell out of favor. Additionally, French doll makers faced stiff competition from German companies, who were often able to meet or exceed the quality of the French dolls at a lower price to consumers. It was no longer feasible for the French manufacturers to continue producing the elaborate Parisiennes and their wardrobes.

Dolls that represented children dominated the market well into the 20th century. During that time, numerous changes revolutionized the doll making industry. The United States replaced war-torn Europe as the hub of toy and doll production. Sophisticated and efficient manufacturing techniques paved the way for the mass production and, subsequently, the mass marketing of dolls. New materials were invented and porcelain and bisque eventually gave way to composition and cellulose, which themselves gave way to hard plastic and vinyl after World War II. Hollywood, which provided Americans with a respite from the Great Depression, also made a huge impact on the doll industry, inspiring the creation of dolls based on child stars such as Shirley Temple, Jane Withers and Margaret O'Brien. About the only thing that had not changed during this time was that dolls were still childlike in proportion and form. Even dolls that were supposed to represent adult women, from brides to fairy tale heroines to *Scarlett O'Hara*, were childlike in proportion and figure, virtually indistinguishable from child dolls when their costumes were removed.

The first deviation from this was an unusual "doll" that was essentially a precursor of the modern-day fashion doll. In the early 1930s through the 1940s, pattern companies such as *Butterick, McCall's* and *Simplicity* marketed miniature, adult female mannequins packaged with patterns, thread and embellishments. The dolls were actually produced by a New York-based company, Latexture Products, Inc., "Manufacturers of Fashiondols (sic)." The original packaging of one such mannequin goes on to say that this is a "Fashiondol (sic) for girls 6 to 60." The impact of that statement cannot be overestimated. Not only does it convey the company's recognition and encouragement of adult play as well as child's play, it is also perhaps the first use of the term "fashion doll" by a manufacturer to describe a modern product. The original packaging further states that this is a mannequin, not a typical doll, and that she is a miniature replica of a teenage girl. Indeed, the figures, proportions and faces were mature, not childlike. The dolls sported high-heeled shoes that were actually part of the leg mold and painted to give an illusion of real shoes. Similarly, the painted hair was also part of the head mold. Unlike traditional dolls, the mannequins were unarticulated except for their arms, which were removable to facilitate dressing the dolls and fitting the patterns. The mannequins came in two sizes, 12-½ inches and 15 inches, and were initially made of hard rubber or rubber-based composition. When the demands of World War II depleted the supply of rubber, the mannequins were made of an early, inflexible plastic. The dolls certainly took on a greater importance during World War II, for self-sufficiency was seen as one's patriotic duty and the dolls were valuable learning tools to teach sewing skills to the wartime generation of girls.

After the World War II, the American doll industry blossomed. Eager to leave behind the sacrifices and horrors of the war, men and women escaped to the suburbs to pursue "The American Dream," and children were an integral part of that dream. The post-war Baby Boom generation was lavished with attention, affection and, of course, an abundance of wonderful toys. Because the economy was robust, parents could indulge their children with things that were inaccessible or simply did not exist when they were children themselves. Consumer demand increased and toy manufacturers were constantly challenged to come up with exciting innovations that would satisfy parents and children alike. And indeed the companies were able to meet the consumers' demands, for the factories that had been dedicated to producing supplies to help win the war turned their efforts to the manufacture of the most wondrous array of consumer goods ever seen. This was the dawn of a golden age of mass produced dolls, with the proliferation of a variety of durable, well-made, affordable dolls. Some were based on popular television personalities such as Mary Hartline and Sherri Lewis and movie stars like Mary Martin and Arlene Dahl. Other dolls portrayed comic strip children such as *Sparkle Plenty* and *Bonnie Braids* from *Dick Tracy*, *Joan Palooka* from the *Joe Palooka* strip and *Li'l Honest Abe* from *Li'l Abner*. Advancements in technology made possible dolls that could walk and the use of nylon made it feasible for dolls such as Ideal's childlike *Toni* to have hair that could be washed, styled and set at home. The same "miracle fibers" that revolutionized doll hair were also utilized in doll clothing, resulting in fashions that were easier to care for and more affordable.

The doll industry was far from alone in undergoing such radical change after World War II. The fashion industry, which had been sorely impacted by the austerity of the war years, was ripe for revitalization, and women embraced frivolous, flirtatious new designs. Rosie the Riveter gladly traded in her overalls and bandanna for the voluminous skirts and tightly corseted waists of Christian Dior's "New Look". This heightened interest in and enthusiasm for fashion was not lost on the doll companies. *Terri Lee*, introduced in 1946, was one of the most fashionable dolls of her time and had an extensive wardrobe of ready-made clothes as well as patterns that were made available so that girls and their mothers could sew their own doll clothes. In 1951, Vogue Dolls introduced a delightful, hard plastic toddler named *Ginny*, "the fashion leader in doll society." That same year, Ideal Toys commissioned 12 French designers such as the House of Worth to create one-of-a-kind gowns for *Toni* dolls that toured upscale department stores around the country. Later, a similar promotion was done with 12 American designers creating more casual fashions for the dolls. Also in 1951, famed designer Elsa Schiaparelli created attire for Effanbee's popular *Honey*, a charming doll that was frequently billed as "A Sweet Child." These limited edition dolls were sold exclusively in the finest stores. The American Character Company entered the fashion doll arena in the early 1950s with *Sweet Sue*, a hard plastic beauty with sleep eyes, hair that could be styled and an enviable wardrobe.

The most influential force in the proliferation of fashionable dolls was Madame Beatrice Alexander, who would irrevocably change the course of fashion doll history. Throughout her doll-making career, Madame had an intense passion for fashion and her creations were exquisitely and stylishly dressed in the finest fabrics available. In 1946, the Alexander Doll Company launched the portrait series, in which sumptuously dressed dolls depicted famous heroines, real and fictional. Five years later, the company produced a hauntingly beautiful series of elaborate creations such as the *Deborah Bride* and the so-called Kathryn Grayson portrait. And in 1953 Madame created a set of 36 dolls for the Abraham & Strauss department store in celebration of the coronation of Queen Elizabeth II. While these dolls were one-of-a-kind and for display only, portraits of Queen Elizabeth and Princess Margaret Rose were available for sale as part of the lavish *Beaux Arts Collection*. Other designs such as the Godey ladies, The *Fashions of a Century* series and *Madeline*, a winsome child doll with a vast wardrobe and a variety of accessories, helped to establish the company's reputation as the premier manufacturer of fashionable dolls. Indeed, Madame Alexander was honored for four consecutive years, 1951 through 1954, with the prestigious Fashion Academy Gold Medal, an honor not specifically for doll makers but rather for the entire fashion industry.

But no matter how adult these dolls appeared while dressed, beneath the sophisticated costumes were the bodies and proportions of children. The heads were large, similar in scale to children's heads, and the feet were flat. The bodies were especially childlike, with slightly chubby waists and the absence of mature breasts. Artful draping and padding of the dolls' garments created the illusion of décolletage on the most fashionable models.

That changed in 1955 with the debut of Alexander's sumptuous *Cissy*, the first articulated, full-figured, high heeled fashion doll. Although *Cissy* sported the childishly large head that had been previously used on the *Winnie* and *Binnie Walkers*, she truly conveyed a womanly appear-

Original box from sewing mannequin. Notice the spelling "fashiondol" (sic). *From the collection of Laura Meisner, photo by James & Meisner.*

Right: Sewing mannequin from late 1930s or early 1940s. *From the collection of Laura Meisner, photo by James & Meisner.*

ance with her arched feet, slim waist and modestly mature bosom. Billed as having "the features of a debutante", *Cissy* was the perfect model for miniature versions of the fabulously feminine fashions of the 1950s. *Cissy* wore "really grown-up" frocks and "never looked prettier" than in her navy taffeta or red dotted Swiss day dresses. Of course, she was a vision in tulle and taffeta in her exquisite evening gowns. However, *Cissy* was not intended to be merely a showpiece or a decorative object; she was meant for children to play with and thus had numerous costumes and accessories, available separately, that would permit imaginative fashion play. While most *Cissy* dolls were sold dressed in day dresses or evening gowns, a basic version dressed in lace undergarments and frilly mules could be purchased as well. Some upscale department stores as well as FAO Schwarz offered elaborate trunk sets consisting of basic dolls and huge, heavily accessorized wardrobes.

As one might guess, *Cissy* was expensive, out of the reach of many consumers. The average *Cissy* doll retailed for approximately $21.95 and

the most ornate versions sold for up to $79.95. By 1956, other doll manufacturers had interpreted the notion of a high-heeled, full-figured fashion doll into less costly, more accessible versions. Ideal introduced *Miss Revlon*, a lovely but somewhat less elaborate doll than *Cissy* that was manufactured in various sizes. *Miss Revlon* had a tie-in to the cosmetic company and a brilliant ad campaign that positioned her as a sort of "big sister" to the child who would play with her. Vogue also played into the big sister theme and came out with *Jill*, the older sibling of their popular *Ginny*. Uneeda created *Dollikin*, a multi-jointed, strung fashion doll whose flexibility mimicked that of a real person. Elsa Schiaparelli re-entered the market, this time in conjunction with Virga, to produce two smaller fashion dolls, *ChiChi* and *GoGo*. Smaller fashion dolls became the rage, and Ideal and Alexander introduced *Miss Revlon* and *Cissette*, diminutive versions of their respective popular creations. Alexander also produced *Elise*, a 16-inch doll with feet jointed at the ankles that could accommodate flats and ballet slippers as well as high heels.

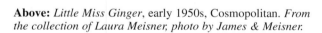

Above: *Little Miss Ginger*, early 1950s, Cosmopolitan. *From the collection of Laura Meisner, photo by James & Meisner.*

Above Right: 22-inch *Miss Revlon*, Ideal, late 1950s. *From the collection of Laura Meisner, photo by James & Meisner.*

Right: *Jill*, Vogue, late 1950s. *From the collection of Laura Meisner, photo by James & Meisner.*

Opposite Page:
Cissy, Alexander Doll Company, mid to late 1950s. *From the collection of Laura Meisner, photo by James & Meisner.*

In addition to the debut of new dolls, several fashionable old favorites were updated. Effanbee's *Honey Walker* suddenly had arched feet and a slimmer figure, and American Character's *Sweet Sue* morphed into *Sweet Sue Sophisticate*. American Character also acquired the license to the name *Toni* from Ideal and reintroduced *Toni* as an utterly charming, mature figured fashion doll in a variety of sizes. In 1957 Cosmopolitan's *Ginny*-like *Ginger* "grew up" and started wearing medium heel "Cha Cha" shoes and in 1958, *Miss Ginger*, a high-heeled version, was introduced.

At the beginning of 1959, the burgeoning fashion doll genre was clearly defined. While there was variety in the size of the dolls, they had several traits in common: arched feet that wore high-heeled shoes, modest but mature bosoms and overscale, childlike heads. Moreover, they shared a similar demeanor; the fashion dolls of the 1950s were demure, prim and perhaps a bit self-effacing, embodying the cultural ideals of upscale femininity of that time. But the debut of Mattel's curvaceous, controversial *Barbie®* doll completely upended the fashion doll world. In stark contrast to her girlish predecessors, the *Barbie®* doll had the unmistakable appearance of an adult woman. She had a smaller head, one that was proportionate for an adult, and dramatic facial painting with blood red lips, severely arched brows and white irises. Her 11-½-inch body was fashioned after the ideal of the 1950s, and she had shapely legs, slim hips, a wasp waist and a full, pointed bosom. Inspired by the German men's novelty Bild *Lilli*, the *Barbie®* doll resembled the popular sex symbols of that time and exuded a similar, blatant sexuality. To be sure, she had more in common with Marilyn Monroe, Jayne Mansfield and Bridgette Bardot than with *Cissy, Jill* or *Miss Revlon*. Furthermore, the *Barbie®* doll's story line was glamorous, for she was a jet-setting fashion model, going on *Roman Holidays* and donning an elegant *Commuter Set* when she went to work. Her "life" was not limited to coffees and cotillions as perhaps *Cissy's* was. Rather, the *Barbie®* doll was a *Career Gal* and had an assertive, almost aggressive air that contrasted markedly with the demure nature of the other fashion dolls.

Consequently, many adults felt that the *Barbie®* doll was inappropriate as a child's plaything. Buyers at the 1959 Toy Fair were unimpressed and parents objected to the doll's mature face and figure. However, while adults dismissed *Barbie®* dolls, children enthusiastically embraced her. They didn't find her severe or exaggerated in the least; rather, she was the epitome of late 1950s glamour and a child's ticket to vicarious participation in the confusing yet compelling world of adults. Moreover, reasonably-priced *Barbie®* dolls were advertised heavily on television and in children's magazines, and they were available almost everywhere. The *Barbie®* doll essentially became a childhood status symbol, the "must have" doll that year. How could indulgent Baby Boom parents, who had always catered to their little darlings' every whim, say no?

By the early 1960s, the *Barbie®* doll's appearance had softened with blue eyes, curved brows and a variety of lip colors and hairstyles. Her pop-

Opposite Page: *Tammy* by Ideal, perhaps the strongest competitor to Mattel's *Barbie®* doll. *From the collection of Glenn Mandeville, photo by Glenn Mandeville.*

Uneeda's *Suzette,* produced in the early 1960s, is a hard-to-find *Barbie®* doll competitor. This one is wearing Mattel's *Friday Nite Date* ensemble. *From the collection of Laura Meisner, photo by James & Meisner.*

Left: *Darci* by Kenner, was a late 1970s competitor. *From the collection of Glenn Mandeville, photo by Glenn Mandeville.*

ularity skyrocketed as more and more children clamored for the high quality doll with the incredible, irresistible wardrobe. Introductions of new characters such as boyfriend *Ken*, best friend *Midge* and little sister *Skipper* kept interest high. Additionally, freckle-faced *Midge* and prepubescent *Skipper* seemed less threatening than *Barbie®* dolls and appealed to those parents who were still put off by the *Barbie®* doll's overt sexuality. Mattel was innovative, interpreting for *Barbie®* dolls and crew the up-to-the-minute trends in clothing, makeup and hair, and coming out with new technologies that would allow the dolls to bend their legs, twist their waists and even talk. The *Barbie®* doll's popularity rose to an unprecedented level and she became the world's most familiar and most loved fashion doll.

However, the *Barbie®* doll's ascent to stardom wreaked havoc on the production and promotion of other fashion dolls. *Cissy*, truly the first contemporary fashion doll, was discontinued after 1959, making but a brief appearance in the portrait series in 1961 and 1962. Alexander's *Cissy*-sized *Jacqueline* doll, named after First Lady Jacqueline Kennedy, was produced in 1961 and 1962; in subsequent years that face was used almost exclusively on portraits. Ideal's *Miss Revlon* disappeared after 1960, and Vogue's *Jill* departed after 1961. *Ginger, Honey* and all the other contenders were gone as well.

Many companies tried to emulate the look — and success — of *Barbie®* dolls. In 1963, American Character, then known as American Doll and Toy Corporation, introduced *Tressy*, a *Barbie®* doll-sized hair play doll with a chic wardrobe and a thick strand of long hair that actually "grew" out of her head. After 1965, *Tressy* was history. Remco Industries, better known for their boys' toys, came out in 1964 with the *Littlechap Family*, which consisted of a well-heeled physician father, his elegant wife and two stylish daughters, *Judy* and *Libby*. These dolls met with a quick demise, in part because they were too large and awkward, with *Judy* towering a full two inches over *Barbie®* dolls, and in part because many consumers could not relate to their rather elitist story line. Ross Products created *Tina Cassini*, a 12-inch teenage fashion doll modeled after the real-life daughter of designer Oleg Cassini and his wife, actress Gene Tierney. Despite a wonderful wardrobe actually created by Oleg Cassini, the doll lasted on the market for less than two years. Even the venerable Alexander Doll Company entered the fray. The cover doll on the company's 1964 catalog was *Brenda Starr*, similar to the *Barbie®* doll in height but with an overscale head, sleep eyes, bendable legs and a more modest figure. The doll was a market failure. In 1965, the company renamed her *Yolanda*,

but she was also unsuccessful.

Ideal Toys produced perhaps the strongest competitors to *Barbie®* dolls. In 1961, they marketed *Mitzi*, who was much like the *Barbie®* doll in face and body shape but ¼-inch taller. In addition, Ideal came out with *Liz*, a 15-inch vinyl fashion doll, and an identical version dubbed *Carol Brent*, which was a special edition for Montgomery Ward. *Liz* was joined for a short time by *Jacqueline*, who was similar in size and shape but had sleep eyes. Ideal's strongest competition for the *Barbie®* doll was 12-inch *Tammy*, a wholesome, winsome teenager with flat feet, an overscale head and merely the slightest hint of a bosom. Produced from 1962 through 1965, *Tammy* was a quality doll with imaginative outfits and accessories and a storyline centering on her family, which appealed to many consumers. In 1965, girlish *Tammy* had a makeover and became more adult in appearance and gained a sophisticated friend, *Misty*, who was also sold as *Glamour Misty, the Miss Clairol doll*. In spite of this, *Tammy* disappeared by the next year. *Misty* fared only slightly better and was "reincarnated" in 1966 and 1967 as *Samantha, the Bewitched Posing Doll*, and in 1967 and 1968 as *Wonder Woman, Super Girl, Batgirl* and *Mera of Atlantis*. With none lasting more than three years, it was clear that no fashion doll could compete with the *Barbie®* doll.

Barbie® dolls redefined fashion dolls and set a new standard by which all others in that genre would be judged. That famous, voluptuous figure and a strict height of 11-½ inches characterized the rigid new standard. Some companies quickly followed suit and pumped out an army of cheap *Barbie®* doll knock-offs that were sold for perhaps a season or two before disappearing into oblivion. Others tried to deviate from the *Barbie®* doll standard but only met with failure. In the early 1970s, Topper met with success with the diminutive *Dawn*, a doll as fashionable and lovely as the *Barbie®* doll but only half her size. For a few years, smaller fashion dolls were all the rage but they fell out of favor by the middle of the decade. Ideal re-entered the fashion doll market in 1974 with its 19-inch *Tiffany Taylor*, who was downsized to 11-½ inches in 1976 and re-named *Tuesday Taylor. Tuesday Taylor*, called *Taylor Jones* in her African-American incarnation, was on the market only until 1978. Kenner came out with *Dusty*, an athletic, androgynous teen doll in 1974, during the heyday of "Women's Lib" when women were struggling to be recognized as people, not merely pretty objects. Despite the progressive social message of *Dusty*, she failed miserably because she was not *Barbie®* doll-sized and because she was aesthetically unappealing to little girls. In the late 1970s, Kenner introduced *Darci*,

Hasbro's *Jem* provided competition for *Barbie*® in the late 1980s.
From the collection of Glenn Mandeville, photo by Glenn Mandeville.

a feminine, multi-jointed 12-½-inch doll with a beautiful face and fashions that accurately reflected the Disco Era. However, she was discontinued in 1981, a victim not only of her nonstandard size but also of the demise of the "disco" lifestyle. Hasbro finally entered the fashion doll arena in 1986 with *Jem,* a well-made, well-designed 12-½-inch doll with a complicated story line. Advertised as *Truly Outrageous, Jem* was a rock star, with glitzy hair and outfits just this side of Madonna and Cyndi Lauper and a cast of characters that would have seemed at home on MTV. Additionally, *Jem* was the star of a weekly children's cartoon show, something Mattel had never

done with the *Barbie*® doll. Yet, *Jem* lasted for only two years. She was replaced by *Maxie,* a similarly sized but more conservative fashion doll with a conventional story line, who fizzled shortly after her debut.

Coming into the 1990s, the *Barbie*® doll had such a stronghold on the fashion doll market that her name practically became synonymous with the genre. So why, in the latter half of the 1990s, did a new standard for adult collectible fashion dolls emerge? To answer that question, we must first take a look at how the *Barbie*® doll herself evolved from plaything to collector's item and how the hobby changed to become what it is today.

Chapter Two

The Birth of a Hobby

The concept of adults collecting fashion dolls was not the brainchild of one individual, not the result of some brilliant marketing campaign, not a phenomenon that suddenly sprang up out of nowhere. Rather, the hobby as it exists today represents an evolution from *Barbie®* doll collecting, which itself grew out of mainstream doll collecting. In order to understand how collectible fashion dolls for adults came to be, it behooves us to recall the beginnings of the organized hobby of doll collecting. We will also take a succinct look

In the Limelight Barbie® doll was a collector edition created for Mattel in the late 1990s by designer Byron Lars.

at the phenomenon of *Barbie®* doll collecting and how it set the stage for the emergence of today's array of fabulous fashion dolls.

Although dolls have existed since the beginning of humanity, it was only relatively recently that the hobby of doll collecting has been seen as a legitimate pastime for adults. Prior to the 20th century, most people thought of dolls only as children's playthings. Indeed there were some exceptions to this, such as the dolls used in some cultures as religious or ceremonial totems or the scandalous, anatomically enhanced dolls created in the late 18th century for the amusement of the French Court. But for the most part, doll collecting by adults did not become popular until the mid 1900s, when the exquisite European dolls of the previous century became valuable, legitimate antiques.

In 1937, Mary E. Lewis and seven like-minded women started the United Federation of Doll Clubs (UFDC), under which most of the doll clubs in the United States have been organized. Incorporated in 1949 with 14 member clubs, the non-profit organization has had as one of its main objectives the promotion of the hobby of collecting dolls. The formation of the UFDC helped legitimize the hobby of collecting dolls and provided a forum under which collectors could network to share discoveries and ideas. However, in the early days of the UFDC, not all dolls were considered collectible. The only dolls deemed worthy of serious attention were the aforementioned antiques such as French fashion dolls and bisque bébés. The mainstream collecting community looked down on the so-called "modern" dolls: the mass-manufactured composition and hard plastic playthings produced in the first half of the 20th century. Still, that did not deter some independent-minded collectors. Many quietly formulated their own definition of "collectible" dolls and began amassing the treasures of their youth. The economy of the late '40s and '50s was good and these collectors were able to afford, for example, the *Shirley Temple* and *Patsy* dolls they may have owned or missed out on in childhood. Moreover, they took notice of the dolls being marketed to their children and grandchildren, including the high-heeled fashion dolls of the mid-1950s. Even though *Cissy, Miss Revlon, Jill* and the rest were marketed as children's toys, these collectors discreetly bought them for themselves, out of appreciation of the quality of the dolls as well as of their sumptuous wardrobes.

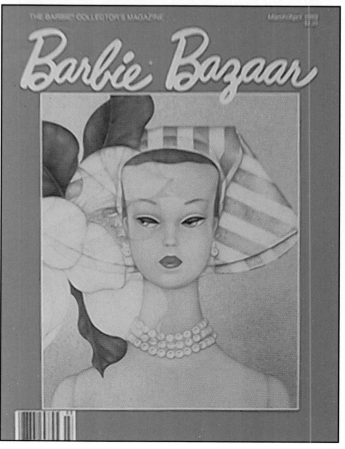

Above: This beautiful side-part *Barbie®* doll from the mid-1960s is highly desirable to collectors. *From the collection of Laura Meisner, photo by James & Meisner.*

Above Right: The *International Barbie®* or *Dolls of the World* series, while intended for children, was popular with adult collectors twenty years ago. It is still one of the most popular series today. This is the first *Native American Barbie®* doll, released in 1993.

Right: An early issue of *Barbie® Bazaar* magazine. This one features a cover illustration by Mel Odom, who would ultimately become the creator of *Gene.* Reprinted with permission of Mel Odom and Marlene Mura.

Naturally, many of these collectors became enchanted with *Barbie®* dolls. They saw parallels between this mass-marketed toy and the wondrous French fashion doll. The *Barbie®* doll, with her realistically-scaled head and slim, mature figure physically resembled the Parisienne more than the childlike, large-headed *Miss Revlon* and *Cissy* did. But the similarities do not stop with physical characteristics. Just as the Parisienne of a hundred years earlier, the *Barbie®* doll had an incredible, sophisticated wardrobe, intricately detailed and fashioned after the cutting-edge styles of the day. She had a wealth of realistic, miniature accessories from purses and gloves to the props of every-day life. And each *Barbie®* doll and outfit was packaged with a fashion booklet, much like the tiny catalogs sometimes given out with the Parisiennes. Indeed, to many of these early, forward-thinking collectors, it was as if the *Barbie®* doll was an affordable, unbreakable, modern-day incarnation of the fabulous French fashion doll. She was no mere plaything; she was an important doll well worth their serious attention.

Others were attracted to the *Barbie®* doll because she was an ideal outlet for their creativity. Home sewing for enjoyment rather than out of necessity was a major pastime in the early years of the *Barbie®* doll's existence and although she was not packaged with patterns like the mannequins of the 1930s and 1940s, commercial patterns were readily available. Many adults who began sewing *Barbie®* doll clothes for their own children or young relatives found this to be a relaxing, satisfying hobby and continued to make *Barbie®* doll garments even when the children in their lives outgrew dolls.

Of course, the first children who played with *Barbie®* dolls did not outgrow them as quickly as youngsters unfortunately do today. *Barbie®* dolls remained popular for them, not as a toy, but as a decorative object. Even teenagers who enjoyed in real life *Friday Nite Dates* and *Junior Prom* continued to buy the beautiful dolls and sophisticated fashions like *Solo in the Spotlight* and *Gold 'N Glamour* to display in their rooms.

In its infancy, the hobby of *Barbie®* doll collecting was a silent, solitary pursuit. There were no adult *Barbie®* doll collector clubs, magazines, reference books or special editions created with the sensibilities of the mature collector in mind. In fact, the mainstream collecting community alternately ignored and disparaged the *Barbie®* doll. The doll wasn't old enough to be antique. She was made of vinyl, not porcelain or bisque. She lacked the cachet of upscale dolls like those made by Madame Alexander. Moreover, she was commonplace, made by the millions for children's play. It is no exaggeration to say that the brave individuals who amassed *Barbie®* dolls were forced underground, keeping their interests mostly to themselves. On those rare occasions in which *Barbie®* dolls were sold at doll shows, it was literally under the table. It was considered poor taste to display a *Barbie®* doll, no matter how rare or beautiful, out in the open on one's sales table.

Barbie® doll collecting began to emerge from that underground in the late 1970s. Several small, mimeographed newsletters were started and the handful of collectors that existed began to network. In 1977, Sibyl DeWein and Joan Ashabraner published the first *Barbie®* doll reference book, *The Collector's Encyclopedia of Barbie® Dolls and Collectibles*. This invaluable work identified and distinguished various dolls, accessories and outfits and imparted a sense of legitimacy to the fledgling hobby, making it easier for *Barbie®* doll collectors to identify themselves as such. The first *Barbie®* doll convention was held in New York

Opposite Page: *1988 Happy Holidays Barbie®* doll caused a furor in the collector world as well as the public at large. *From the collection of Glenn Mandeville, photo by Glenn Mandeville.*

The porcelain nostalgic reproduction *Barbie®* dolls were among the first offerings marketed toward adult collectors in the late 1980s and early 1990s. This is a porcelain reproduction of *Barbie's® Best Friend, Midge.*

City in 1980 and attracted slightly less than 100 collectors. Ruth Cronk, who had started the popular *Barbie® Gazette* newsletter in the spring of 1977, chaired the event.

The acceptability of the *Barbie®* doll as a legitimate collectible grew slowly but steadily through the 1980s. In the mid-80s, the UFDC officially recognized the collectibility of modern dolls and created competition categories specifically for them. In an article for *Barbie® Bazaar*, noted doll authority A. Glenn Mandeville wrote that as a UFDC judge he was "pleasantly surprised" to see collectors who had just placed dolls worth thousands in the antique competition come into the modern competition room with *Barbie®* dolls. Mattel began to acknowledge the existence of the collector as well. In 1981, the company launched its first collectible series, the *International Barbie® Dolls* (later, *Dolls of the World*), a kaleidoscope of ethnically accurate dolls in various interpretations of traditional dress. While this series was intended for children, it was wildly popular among adult collectors. Eventually, Mattel created its first *Barbie®* doll specifically for adults, the porcelain *Blue Rhapsody Barbie®*, which was previewed at the 1986 convention. While some collectors objected to a *Barbie®* doll made out of any material but vinyl, the response was positive enough to justify the issue of more porcelain creations, including classic dolls in reproductions of favorite nostalgic fashions. Finally, the public began to take serious notice of *Barbie®* dolls in 1984, when designer BillyBoy* created the *New Theater of Fashion,* a travelling exhibit of international haute couture in which the doll served as both mannequin and muse. Inspired by *Le Petit Théâtre de la Mode,* the exhibit, intended as a tribute to the *Barbie®* doll for her 25th anniversary, was later chronicled by BillyBoy* in his book, *Barbie® Her Life and Times.* Not only did this book showcase the creativity the doll could inspire, it also provided entertaining tidbits and anecdotes about her history that made many people take a closer look at this "child's toy." In 1987, *Feelin' Groovy Barbie®,* a department store exclusive designed by BillyBoy*, generated excitement among adult collectors, even those focused on pre-1972 "vintage" dolls, and proved that indeed there was a market for vinyl *Barbie®* dolls that catered to adult tastes.

The years 1988 through 1993 were pivotal in the growing hobby of *Barbie®* doll collecting. *Barbie® Bazaar*, the first glossy magazine dedicated to promoting the hobby and disseminating news and information to the adult collector, debuted in 1988. Published by Karen Caviale and Marlene Mura, *Barbie® Bazaar* was a groundbreaking force in legitimizing and popularizing *Barbie®* doll collecting. Sleek and professional, the magazine's beginnings were surprisingly humble; it literally came to life on an Apple computer in the basement of Caviale's parents' home through the efforts of Caviale, Mura and their families and friends. With articles about *Barbie®* doll clubs and stories by and about adult enthusiasts, *Barbie® Bazaar* was instrumental in creating a community of collectors. Isolated individuals who chanced upon *Barbie® Bazaar* realized that they were not the only adults who enjoyed, amassed and appreciated this little vinyl doll and many became active and eager participants in the burgeoning fellowship of *Barbie®* doll collectors. In addition, *Barbie® Bazaar* imbued a sense of respectability to the hobby by regularly publishing serious reference articles that classified and showed variations in vintage dolls, fashions and accessories. Moreover, the magazine broadened collectors' horizons by covering foreign market editions, vintage as well as contemporary, and provided a singular source for news and information regarding upcoming releases, collectibles and play line alike.

The other significant event of 1988 was the first *Barbie®* doll frenzy with the issue of the premiere *Happy Holidays Barbie®*. Although she was the most expensive vinyl *Barbie®* doll to date, with a retail price of $39.99, the doll literally flew off store shelves and was already hard to find by October of that year. The ensuing furor was not unlike the one brought about in 1983 by the introduction of *Cabbage Patch Kids.* Consumers camped in their cars before stores opened and spent entire days going from store to store in search of the doll. Unfortunately, many dolls were scooped up by speculators who were interested not in *Barbie®* dolls but in making quick profits and secondary market prices soared to $1,000 in some places the week before Christmas. Since Christmas 1988 of course the secondary market values have abated.

In 1989, the 30th anniversary of the *Barbie®* doll brought more attention from the public. In a day in which most toys were popular for only a few years, the *Barbie®* doll's 30-year tenure as the world's preeminent fashion doll was truly remarkable. Naturally the media picked up on this, and serious journalists engaged in intellectual analysis of the doll on national television and in mainstream publications. As interest in *Barbie®* dolls grew, companies received licenses from Mattel to produce items such as jewelry, T-shirts, greeting cards and coffee mugs. It became more commonplace to see vintage as well as some new *Barbie®* items at doll shows as the stigma attached to collecting the doll had, thankfully, vanished.

Moreover, during this time, the Baby Boomers who had first played with *Barbie®* dolls were themselves coming of age. Many began collecting the doll as a way to return to a simpler time, to re-experience the joy they felt as children and to share with their own children something beloved from their past. Those who were denied the doll because of age, gender or parental objections treated themselves to a childhood experience on which they had missed out. To be sure, some of the most avid *Barbie®* doll collectors were men who were often not permitted to play with dolls as boys or women whose parents gave them demure fashion dolls like *Tammy,* knock-offs like *Babs* or child dolls like *Penny Brite.* Additionally, the adult Boomers had considerable spending power. Established in their careers, many had enough disposable income that they could buy the vintage treasures from their youth, which were still fairly affordable, and yet have enough money left over for the few collector editions issued each year.

The first half of the 1990s was clearly the heyday of contemporary *Barbie®* dolls as collectibles. Mattel began issuing more editions targeted toward adults: the company continued and expanded its line of porcelain dolls and evolved *Happy Holidays Barbie®* into a series. In 1990, the first *Barbie®* doll designed by Bob Mackie debuted. The suggested retail price of the vinyl doll was steep at the time, $125, and sales were rather slow until the introduction of two more Mackie creations the following year. Collectors

Customized dolls became wildly popular in the mid-1990s among avid *Barbie®* doll enthusiasts who were looking to add something a little different to their collections. *Tropical Splash Christie* was made over by the talented team of Bruce Nygren and Peter Nickel.

realized that the designer dolls were a trend, not an aberration, and quickly backtracked to get that ever-important first doll in the series at retail price. In 1992 Mattel introduced its *Classique* series to spotlight its in-house designers and in 1993, the *Great Eras* series debuted, interpreting the *Barbie®* doll as a timeless icon, from an ancient Egypt queen to a 20th Century Flapper. Special edition dolls were created for a diverse market, from upscale chains like FAO Schwarz to discount and grocery stores to the cable TV home shopping channels.

By the *Barbie®* doll's 35th anniversary in 1994, the heyday was giving way to sheer havoc. As more collectors entered the hobby, competition for vintage items dramatically increased, causing prices to escalate past the point at which many could afford the more elusive items. But while there was a finite supply of vintage items, the stream of new dolls issued each year seemed endless. Whereas there had previously been a smattering of collector edition dolls each year, suddenly the consumer was inundated with more designer dolls, new series such as *Hollywood Legends* and the vinyl nostalgic reproductions, more retailer exclusives and more licensed merchandise. In terms of contemporary collectibles, *Barbie®* doll enthusiasts had truly gone from famine beyond feast and many felt overwhelmed and burned out by the sheer number of options from which they had to choose.

The mainstream media attention surrounding *Barbie®* dolls was partly responsible for the frenzy of the mid-90s. While it was good in that it introduced *Barbie®* doll collecting as a legitimate pastime, it was harmful in that much inaccurate information was disseminated, creating a false impression that regardless of age or condition, any *Barbie®* doll was literally worth her weight in gold. An example of this type of misleading article appeared in the February 1995 issue of *Reader's Digest*. A headline on the front of the magazine screamed, "Cash In On Today's Collectibles" and the article inside, entitled *Money in Your Attic*, showed a played-with contemporary *Barbie®* doll with cut, frizzy hair, dressed in frayed satin shorts and a nondescript flowered shirt. Incredibly, underneath this picture was the question, "$1500 for a *Barbie®* doll?" Later in the article, it was explained that an "original" *Barbie®* doll could be worth $1,500, but there was no illustration or explanation as to what constituted that originality or determined the price. Articles like this prompted many to scour their basements, attics and children's toy boxes in search of "valuable" dolls. While indeed some unearthed real treasures that were desirable to collectors, others erroneously saw gold in their dolls with broken hips, missing fingers and ears turned green from earrings as well as their ubiquitous blonde *SuperStars* from the late 1970s and on.

Moreover, the sudden interest in the value of old *Barbie®* dolls increased mass speculative buying and hoarding of new products. The 1988 *Happy Holidays Barbie®* brouhaha was a lesson well learned by many, who bought not one or two of each subsequent doll in the series, but one or two CASES of each. Stores, wanting to satisfy their customers, substantially increased their orders. Additionally, all stores wanted "in" on the *Barbie®* doll boom and upscale collector dolls that had been the mainstay of small doll shops began to appear on the shelves of grocery stores and discount chains like Wal-Mart. However, dolls were never on the shelves for very long. Speculators often ordered dolls from several shops, cruised the malls and filled their carts at Toys "R" Us, literally scooping up all the available dolls in their area. As a result, frustrated collectors felt forced to pay the scalpers' inflated prices because they could not find the dolls on store shelves. As a result, many of them also began hoarding and speculating. It was not unheard of for collectors to scoop up a store's entire inventory of *35th Anniversary* brunettes or *Barbie®* as Scarlett O'Hara dolls—and go back a few days later to look for more.

Another trend that proved devastating to *Barbie®* doll collecting was the obsession with keeping dolls in their boxes. Much of that widespread mindset stemmed from the appreciation in

Benefit Ball Barbie® doll, designed by Carol Spencer, was the first in Mattel's popular *Classique* series.

37

The stunning popularity of Ty Company's *Beanie Babies* impacted adversely upon the mainstream popularity of collectable *Barbie®* dolls. *The End* is from 1999.

value of vintage items; a Never Removed From Box (NRFB) 1959 *Barbie®* doll, for example, commanded far more than a doll in similar condition without its original packaging. However, because vintage items were intended to be children's toys, the few which survived NRFB throughout all those years were truly rare and precious. The collector of contemporary *Barbie®* dolls kept them in boxes, thinking that they, too, would someday be as valuable as the vintage items. However, that logic was flawed because thousands of other collectors were thinking exactly the same thing, squirreling away their boxed collectibles in closets and under beds. Whereas yesterday's NRFB doll is a rarity, today's boxed collector edition may be commonplace in the future, especially if supply outpaces demand. The NRFB mentality had other dire consequences on *Barbie®* doll collecting. Many collectors were genuinely afraid to take their dolls out of box, lest they lose their value. As a result, they sacrificed much of the joy of collecting and some even dropped out, saying that the hobby was no longer fun. Others bought two identical dolls, one to keep in the box and one to take out to display, a practice that quickly added expense to one's doll budget. Some collectors took that notion a step further and bought extra dolls for the purpose of trading or

selling them. Attics and basements filled with boxed dolls and collectors frantically juggled credit cards, tried to outsmart the scalpers and attempted in vain to keep up with every new series and all the new dolls released each year.

By 1996, the *Barbie®* doll collecting fad began to fizzle. To meet its unprecedented consumer demand, Mattel furiously increased production numbers. However, that demand was artificial, created by speculators, hoarders and collectors who bought en masse; thus it appeared that the customer base for such products was far greater than it actually was. Consequently, the market was flooded and the demand decreased abruptly. Collectors were dismayed to find dolls for which they had paid full price not six months earlier sitting on clearance shelves in discount stores or hawked on cable shopping channels for a fraction of what they originally paid. Hoards of speculators dumped their previously purchased doll "investments," causing a decline in some secondary market prices.

Contributing to the meltdown, a new craze had captured the hearts and wallets of Americans. The meteoric rise in popularity of Ty Company's *Beanie Babies* was another significant blow to the *Barbie®* frenzy. Lured by the promise that a five-dollar toy might fetch a quick return of hundreds, if not thousands, of dollars, speculators and scalpers swarmed to *Beanie Babies*. Groupies who were interested only in collecting what was currently "hot" also moved on, as did some die-hard *Barbie®* doll enthusiasts, who recaptured the "thrill of the chase" in scouring the malls and the Internet for *Beanies* just as they did for the 1988 *Happy Holidays Barbie®*. Moreover, the media lost interest in *Barbie®* dolls and turned their attention to *Beanie Babies*. Camera crews, national as well as local, chronicled the waiting lines and the fistfights that broke out in shops that had too few desirable *Beanies* to satisfy their frantic customers. Mainstream newspapers and magazines that previously examined the *Barbie®* doll hobby started to run features about the *Beanie* phenomenon. Magazines about general collectibles such as *White's Guide to Collecting Figures* replaced the *Barbie®* dolls that used to grace their covers with the most desirable *Beanies* of the moment. Reference guides sprang up overnight and a seemingly endless stream of *Beanie Baby* magazines appeared on newsstands everywhere. The *Barbie®* doll was no longer the apple of the fickle public eye and chaos and confusion reigned as the *Barbie®* doll market struggled to correct itself.

In the midst of that chaos, a new doll emerged, one that would change fashion doll collecting as radically as the *Barbie®* doll herself changed fashion doll play when she was introduced. That radical new doll was *Gene*.

Chapter Three

The Harbingers of Change

Before the debut of *Gene*, several innovative creations hit the market in the late 1980s and early 1990s that set the stage for the birth of this whole new genre of collectible fashion dolls. *Mdvanii* by BillyBoy*, *Lady Luminous* by Takara and the *American Models* by Robert Tonner challenged fashion doll enthusiasts to expand their horizons beyond *Barbie®* dolls. Concurrently, the

Alexander Doll Company was slowly bringing *Cissy* back into the collective consciousness with a smattering of special editions that hinted at the sumptuous makeover the doll would receive in the mid-90s. We shall focus this chapter on these *avant-garde* dolls.

In 1989, BillyBoy*, well known among *Barbie®* doll enthusiasts for his groundbreaking

Gold Lamé, an *American Model* from 1994, Robert Tonner Doll Company. *From the collection of Laura Meisner, photo by James & Meisner.*

contributions to the hobby, introduced his own unique fashion doll vision. *Mdvanii*, a 10-inch doll made of resin, was the first modern-day fashion doll to explore the world of upscale haute couture. Inspired by the classic silhouettes of the 1940s, 1950s and 1960s, her sophisticated costumes were meticulously made out of fine materials such as Dupioni silk, Harris tweed and Liberty of London prints. She wore interchangeable wigs made of human hair and each doll's face was painted by hand. Additionally, she was lavishly accessorized with perfectly scaled jewelry, mirrors, handbags, perfume bottles and other necessities for her well-heeled "life." Later, other characters were introduced in the *Mdvanii* line. *Dheei* was an elegant woman of color made from a unique face mold. *Soraya* was an Indian character, said to be "psychic." *Edie*, *Mdvanii's* younger sister, had a Mod-inspired wardrobe and flat feet. The line was further enhanced with the addition of several male friends, such as *Rhogit-Rhogit*, a Caucasian man, and *Zhdrick*, who was black.

Unfortunately, there were drawbacks to the *Mdvanii* dolls. The dolls were extremely expensive at a time when vintage *Barbie®*dolls were still relatively affordable. An advertisement in the January/February 1990 issue of *Barbie® Bazaar* lists a "Dress Up" doll wearing only a foundation garment for $195. A later ad, in the September/October 1991 issue, shows "The New Basic" *Mdvanii*, dressed in a choice of elegant, retro-inspired sheaths, for $500. According to an article by Pat Henry in the June 1999 issue of *The FashionDoll Scene*, some gift sets commanded prices up to $3,000. Additionally, *Mdvanii* was hard to find. In the United States, the dolls were first carried by Bloomingdale's and then by FAO Schwarz as well as a handful of small doll shops. In her article, Henry further stated that no one store or retailer carried the entire line. Thus, even collectors who could afford the dolls found it daunting to obtain what they wanted. Moreover, the dolls were fragile. The resin used in their manufacture proved to be brittle over time and occasionally the dolls broke at the wrists or ankles when collectors attempted to redress them.

The *Mdvanii* line was also fraught with controversy. The dolls were anatomically correct, which pleased some consumers but offended others. Furthermore, the male dolls were marketed with a "safe sex" theme. An ad in the March/April 1993 issue of *Barbie® Bazaar* proclaims that *Rhogit-Rhogit's* twin, *Timky*, "comes with a condom, like his brother, because he, like all dolls in *Mdvanii's* world, believes, regardless of your preference, it is imperative to practice safe sex." To be sure, some collectors saw this as a courageous, timely and appropriate statement, but others viewed it as a distasteful, perhaps unnecessary,

intrusion of sexuality into the fantasy world of fashion dolls.

In an article in the August/September 1999 issue of *Miller'$ Fashion Doll*, Doris Mixon stated that BillyBoy* withdrew his creations from the American market but that *Mdvanii* is still being marketed in Europe and Japan. Although several resin one-of-a-kind dolls are shown in the article, BillyBoy* said that current *Mdvanii* dolls are handmade in Europe of French porcelain. He also said that he is not averse to creating a "more accessible" *Mdvanii* doll for today's collectors. Certainly the notion of a new incarnation of *Mdvanii* is intriguing and it behooves the avid collector to keep abreast of any possible developments.

Another doll that was ahead of her time was Takara's *Lady Luminous*, also known as *Deux-L*. Introduced in 1988 for the Japanese collectors' market, the hauntingly beautiful *Lady Luminous* had a realistic appearance that contrasted markedly with Takara's charmingly cartoonish *Jenny*, a *Barbie®* doll-sized play doll for children. At 17 inches tall, *Lady Luminous* was one-quarter the size of the ideal human fashion model, and her measurements were proportionate and natural, not exaggerated in the least. Her body was tastefully sculpted with the delicate delineation of a clavicle, a navel and nipples. *Lady Luminous* sported a variety of hair colors and styles and she was available in three skin colors: stark white, brown and suntan. Her clothing, which was sold separately, accurately reflected mid-80s couture, with suits, day dresses, bridal gowns and even a real mink coat comprising her wardrobe.

Lady Luminous was extremely popular in Japan, especially with men who bought the dolls in model shops and customized them by repainting the faces and creating clothes and jewelry of their own design. However, her appeal was somewhat limited in the United States. One reason is that she was hard to find. While some shops imported the doll from Japan, she was not widely distributed on the American market. Furthermore, she was expensive, with basic dressed dolls retailing between $195 and $225 and costumes selling for $68 on up. More elaborate dolls, such as the brides and the versions draped in genuine mink, were even costlier. Another reason for the lukewarm reception to the doll by U.S. collectors was her lack of articulation. Jointed only at the neck and shoulders, *Lady Luminous* was forever frozen in the classic model's stance, with one leg slightly bent and ahead of the other. Although this look was aesthetically pleasing, it gave the impression that this was truly a "petite mannequin" rather than a doll with which the collector could interact. This absence of "character," combined with a size that was, at the time, too large and too different for

Mint in box basic *Mdvanii* doll by BillyBoy*. *From the collection of J. Douglas James, photo by James & Meisner.*

Mint in box original *Mdvanii* outfit. *From the collection of J. Douglas James, photo by James & Meisner.*

most U.S. collectors, doomed this luminous lady to near obscurity. By 1993, production of the doll ceased. Again the question must be raised: Would a revamped, perhaps more posable *Lady Luminous* meet with greater acceptance by collectors today?

Fortunately for today's collectors, an idea that was not ahead of its time was the *American Model Collection* by Robert Tonner. A former Seventh Avenue fashion designer, Tonner was already a doll artist of renown, respected and admired for exquisite one-of-a-kind creations and extremely limited editions, when he launched his own company in the early 1990s. Tonner was (and still is!) unique in the doll world for his ability to capture the magic of childhood in winsome, utterly delightful child dolls as well as interpret the elegance and glamour of haute couture in his adult fashion dolls. Tonner's first fashion dolls were created out of porcelain. Approximately 17 inches tall, his original models had 13 leather-lined ball socket joints, giving them an almost lifelike posability. In 1992, Tonner made his debut at Toy Fair, offering a child doll as well as a porcelain fashion model in six different ensembles. These were very limited and very expensive, priced at $1,500 or more. In 1993, Tonner introduced his first vinyl doll, *Kaylie*, an adorable child doll in upscale, classic little girls' fashions. That year, he released only one porcelain model, sold with a trunk of clothing.

In retrospect, it now seems only logical that Tonner's next innovation would be his own vinyl fashion doll. Indeed, in 1994, he introduced his

American Model Collection, a line of beautifully sculpted adult dolls dressed in classic yet contemporary couture. Although the models were not as posable as the earlier porcelain incarnations, they were produced in larger editions and were much more affordable, priced at approximately $300. That first year, individual outfits were available separately, priced between $69.95 and $89.95. These fashion dolls were statuesque, standing 19 inches tall. When asked why they were that particular size, Tonner explained that he didn't want to compete with *Barbie®* dolls. He felt that Mattel had done such a superlative job in creating an 11-½-inch fashion doll that he didn't see a need to follow suit. Rather, he had his own vision, one of a fashion doll with realistic proportions and an athletic, contemporary ideal, not the exaggerated '50s feminine form as seen on *Barbie®* dolls.

The *American Models* were embraced enthusiastically by mainstream doll enthusiasts, who saw them as a marriage of fashion and fine doll art in a user-friendly form. However, the fashion doll world, still fixated on *Barbie®* dolls at that time, was slower to warm up to something so completely different. Nevertheless, the *American Models* have consistently remained popular, an integral part of the ever-evolving Tonner line, with new collectors drawn to them each day. But the *American Models*, for all their elegance and sophistication, did not represent the pinnacle of Tonner's fashion doll vision. As we shall see later, the best was yet to come.

While Robert Tonner was blazing new trails in

Below: Takara's *Lady Luminous* piqued the interest of U.S. fashion doll collectors in the late 1980s.

Above: *Lady Luminous* was available in three skin colors, white, black and suntan. The white version, shown here, is literally paper white.

This is one of the first multi-jointed porcelain fashion dolls done by Robert Tonner. *Photo courtesy of the Robert Tonner Doll Company.*

Below: Four more of Tonner's exquisite porcelain fashion model dolls done prior to his vinyl creations. *Photo courtesy of the Robert Tonner Doll Company.*

the fashion doll world, the Madame Alexander Doll Company was resurrecting an old favorite. In 1990, after a 30-year absence, *Cissy* was back. A limited edition for FAO Schwarz, *Cissy* was dressed in an ensemble designed by Arnold Scaasi, a favorite designer of former First Lady Nancy Reagan. In many ways, this *Cissy* was a hybrid, an interesting mix of old and new. She had the same face and body sculpt as did vintage *Cissy*. Her makeup was subtle and understated, very similar to what it was in the 1950s. Yet, there were differences. Unlike her vintage predecessor, this *Cissy* had a vinyl head instead of one made of hard plastic, giving her a somewhat softer, warmer appearance. The sleeve-jointed arms were replaced with elegant, slender one-piece arms. And although it was the same face mold as vintage, this new incarnation of *Cissy* had more closely spaced eyes. The holes cut to accommodate *Cissy's* sleep-eyes were slightly larger. Additionally, she sported unusual, bee-stung lips that some collectors found endearing but others found unappealing. After that initial debut, the

hybrid *Cissy* made several more appearances. In 1991, she was used as the *Enchanted Evening* Portrait; essentially the identical doll as the earlier FAO exclusive, she was draped in aqua chiffon and crystals. And in 1993 and 1994, she was the winsome, brunette *Lilac Fairie Ballerina*.

The early 1990s were a time of experimentation with the design and persona of *Cissy*. The cover of the 1993 Madame Alexander catalog shows a one-of-a-kind creation made for auction at the 1992 Walt Disney World Doll & Teddy Bear convention. This lavishly designed *Cissy* had the bee-stung lips of the FAO exclusive and the portraits, yet she sported large, feathered eyebrows and sumptuous red hair. Her Victorian-era gown was padded to give the illusion of a larger, fuller bosom. There was even a porcelain *Cissy* produced from 1993 to 1994. The *Cissy Godey Bride* was unlike any other *Cissy*, with brilliant blue glass inset eyes, long lashes, a deep brunette wig and unique facial painting.

All through this time, the Alexander Doll Company was in a state of profound change. With faith that her legacy would be continued, Madame Alexander sold the company in 1988 to Ira Smith and Jeff Chodorow, two businessmen. Although hopes were high when the company changed hands, in a few years it seemed to many collectors that the company simply was not the same as it had been with Madame at the helm. Her death in 1990, at the age of 95, deepened those sentiments. Meanwhile, the company explored new creative ventures and attempted to diversify with associations with doll artists such as Hildegard Günzel and Robin Woods. Ultimately, these affiliations were discontinued by 1995. The once venerable company suffered severe financial setbacks in the early 1990s, and it was sold in 1995 to the Kaizen Breakthrough Partnership. As the new owners and management worked to overcome the company's financial woes and restore Madame's legacy, a design team led by John Puzewski was developing yet another step in the evolution of *Cissy*. And, just like with Robert Tonner's fashion doll creations, the best was again yet to come.

The legacy of these innovative, unique dolls was that they truly broadened collectors' horizons and facilitated the acceptance of the doll that would revolutionize the hobby and be the standard-bearer of the new genre in collectible fashion dolls. In our next chapter, we'll take an in-depth look at the revolutionary in high heels, the lovely *Gene*.

The Alexander Doll Company reintroduced *Cissy* after a 30-year hiatus. This advertisement shows the first contemporary incarnation of *Cissy*, dressed by Arnold Scaasi and sold exclusively by FAO Schwarz in 1990.

Opposite Page: The *Enchanted Evening Portrait* was essentially the same doll as the FAO exclusive Scaasi but dressed in this diaphanous blue gown.

Chapter 4

Share the Dream

Life's romance is taking the chance
To follow the dream in your heart
It's up to you to make it come true
Wish on the highest star

Share the dream, share the dream
Be all that you can be
And let love be the theme
Believe and share the dream

From *Share the Dream*
(Gene's Theme)
©1999 Ashton-Drake Galleries

Some revolutions begin with a bang and others begin with a whisper. The revolution that rocked the fashion doll world began with a dream, the dream of an avid collector to create his own doll, one that embodied the best qualities of other fashionable dolls he admired interspersed with childhood memories of glamour and sophistication as interpreted by the silver screen. That collector shared his dream with the fashion doll world and changed the hobby forever. That collector, of course, was Mel Odom and his dream was *Gene*.

The dream that became *Gene Marshall* began rather modestly with Odom's childhood love of dolls. He has fond memories of the dolls that peppered his early life, from the dolls handed down by older girl cousins to the *Peter Pan* doll that helped alleviate his anxiety on the first day of school. The *Barbie*® doll played an important role in Odom's childhood. He owned a *Ken* doll and later purchased a titian bubble cut *Barbie*® doll. "I really

Midnight Romance Gene was an exclusive for mail order retailers in 1997.
Photo courtesy of Ashton-Drake.

wanted the white ginger platinum bubble cut, but my mother thought she looked 'cheap.' So I went for class instead. Hey, I didn't mind. I felt lucky just to be getting a *Barbie®* doll." Odom spent many hours in creative, interactive doll play. "My *Barbie®* doll didn't live the life of leisure like some dolls do. She had adventures! Sometimes she would be Fay Wray in the clutches of King Kong and sometimes she would be Arlene Dahl being chased by dinosaurs like in *Journey to the Center of the Earth.* My *Barbie®* doll was prone to be attacked by monsters and didn't just pose and look pretty. She was in the action." Odom remembers also how his *Barbie®* doll didn't wear the fancier gowns that were available then. "All of the clothes I bought for her were tailored, like the *Knitting Pretty* sweater outfit that came with a bowl of yarn and her shopping dress with the big, broad hat, *Suburban Shopper.* I preferred real looking clothes for her."

Odom's childhood experiences with his beloved *Barbie®* doll were a tremendous influence on the ultimate creation of *Gene.* Contact with the actual people behind *Barbie®* dolls also made an impact on him. Before the debut of *Fashion Queen Barbie®* and *Miss Barbie®*, two versions of the popular doll that were sold with wigs, he had written to Mattel specifically requesting such a doll. Odom was thrilled to receive a reply from a Mattel employee, and, years later, when he met the *Barbie®* doll's creator, Ruth Handler, he related to her how much that meant to him. To this day, he speaks respectfully and admiringly of Handler. "There was a lot of love in those first *Barbie®* dolls. They weren't just products; they were special. She even named those dolls after her own two children." Similarly, *Gene* is imbued with a deep sense of affection and respect and to Odom, she is not "just a product." Rather, *Gene* reflects his desire to touch collectors' hearts the way that Handler and her creation touched his.

Another influence that led to Odom's eventual creation of *Gene* was the presence of dolls in his adult life. The first "doll" he purchased preceded his collection by several years. On a whim, Odom bought a 21-inch composition mannequin in the early 1970s. "I saw her in an antique shop in Virginia, wearing this pink and white *I Love Lucy* housedress, and I could not resist her. I took her to England with me and traveled with her." Odom believes that his mannequin, whom he named Vera, was used in the late 1930s or 1940s as a *Simplicity* display piece in fabric stores to show women what finished garments made from the different patterns would look like. "She's larger than the sewing mannequins that were sold for children at that time. She's really too large for a child to handle well. I believe Vera was the last of the 'working' fashion dolls in that she was used to demonstrate fashions, just like the fashion dolls of

years ago." Vera holds a special place in Odom's heart. "I loved that period she was from, the fashions, the styles. And she was proportioned like a human, not so much like a doll. She truly has the presence of a person; when you look at her from across a room, it's like looking at a person who is standing far away." For several years, Vera was the only doll in Odom's adult life. "She stood by herself for a long time. My friend Tim Kennedy used to make clothes for her." In time, a similar mannequin, a suntanned version that was perhaps used to model swimwear, and an array of other fashionable dolls joined Vera, turning her into the matriarch of a full-fledged collection. But perhaps more importantly, Vera was the first doll that served as Odom's artistic muse and was indeed an important influence in his eventual creation of *Gene.*

Barbie® dolls came back into Odom's life through his career. A successful and well-known freelance illustrator, Odom was inspired to pay homage to what he felt was an overlooked American pop culture icon, the *Barbie®* doll. One of his *Barbie®* doll drawings appeared in a 1983 issue of *Playboy* and resulted in Odom receiving fan letters from adult *Barbie®* doll collectors. The art director at *Playboy* began searching for *Barbie®* dolls at flea markets to give to Odom, and before long, the illustrator had an impressive collection. Odom's interest in *Barbie®* dolls also led to a friendship with BillyBoy* and involvement in the *New Theater of Fashion.* Odom contributed several portraits of *Barbie®* dolls as well as a customized doll that represented the mythical Daphne, a nymph who was changed into a laurel tree. A photo of that doll appeared in the March 1989 issue of *Barbie® Bazaar,* a publication for which Odom had created several illustrations, two of which were featured on the magazine's covers.

However, Odom became restless within the confines of his collection. He frequently repainted other fashion dolls, such as *Lady Luminous,* for his own enjoyment, but he wanted something more. "I couldn't get exactly what I wanted just by repainting existing dolls." At this same time, BillyBoy* was immersed in the creation of *Mdvanii.* Odom found the observation of his friend's experience to be quite inspirational. "I used to think that only a corporation could make a fashion doll, but watching BillyBoy* made me realize that an individual could do it as well." Thus the spark that became *Gene* was ignited. In 1991, Odom drew a portrait of a woman who immediately blossomed into a character in his mind. He developed a story line for his character, one that revolved around the beloved silver screen idols of the 1940s and 1950s that colored his childhood. He showed his picture of *Gene* to friends and colleagues, and was encouraged by their positive responses to take his dream to fruition.

One of Mel Odom's inspirations in the creation of *Gene* was a mannequin he dubbed "Vera", shown here in a fan magazine that accompanied *Gene's Afternoon Off* ensemble.

Mattel's *Barbie®* doll was another major inspiration in the creation of *Gene*. Here is the second Odom illustration to appear on the cover of *Barbie® Bazaar* magazine. Reprinted with permission of Mel Odom and Marlene Mura.

At this same time, Odom had come to a crossroads in his career. Although very successful as an illustrator, he no longer felt challenged and recognized the need to make a significant change. "I saw this time as a fork in the road. If I had not done *Gene*, I would have gone into painting. However, the world has many painters. I think I was the only person who could have created *Gene*." As an avid collector, Odom's need to create the doll of his dreams was immediate and he put on hold his desires to pursue painting. "I thought of *Gene* as something to which I could devote a number of years of my life and I'd still be able to paint later."

Of course, Odom realized that it would take the efforts of many people to bring his dream to fruition. Michael Evert, a freelance sculptor who had previously created mannequins for Pucci, was tapped to translate Odom's drawings of *Gene* into three-dimensional form. Odom's longtime friends Tim Kennedy, Timothy Alberts and Doug James, talented gentlemen who designed clothes for real people, agreed to create *Gene's* wardrobe. Alberts also made elaborate wigs for the plaster *Gene* prototypes. Later, when it was decided that the doll would be rooted rather than wigged, Laura Meisner, a talented stylist and doll restoration expert, joined the team to coif *Gene's* hair. And when several successful prototypes of *Gene* had been created, Odom approached the Ashton-Drake Galleries to forge with them an agreement to manufacture and distribute his doll. Shortly after Ashton-Drake signed the agreement with Odom, product development expert Joan Greene was hired and ultimately became the project's corporate champion.

Gene made her official debut at Toy Fair 1995, with a gala event at the Plaza Hotel that formally introduced her to her fans. However, *Gene*, was almost ahead of her time, for her premiere occurred at the peak of the *Barbie®* doll collecting frenzy. Although *Gene* was created by a collector with adult tastes and sensibilities in mind, the hobby was still so focused on *Barbie®* dolls that it was a formidable challenge to broaden fashion doll enthusiasts' horizons enough to accept *Gene*. Moreover, *Gene's* larger size and her unusual, stylized appearance initially put off many would-be enthusiasts.

Gene's then-unconventional size was a stroke of creative brilliance. As much as Odom admired *Barbie®* dolls, he intended *Gene* to be unique, not an imitation of *Barbie®* dolls. He did a full-length drawing of his concept of *Gene* and reproduced it in various sizes, finally deciding on 15-½ inches as the most aesthetically pleasing. *Gene's* clothing designers assured Odom that the size was optimal for dressmaking, pointing out that many of the French fashion dolls were that size. Incidentally, many of the sewing mannequins of the 1930s and 1940s were about that size as well. The size proved to be ideal for the collector; much larger would render the doll a bit difficult to handle and to display while much smaller would make her hard to dress and stifle interactivity. Coincidentally, 15-½-inch *Gene* fit into an adult's hand much the way the 11-½-inch *Barbie®* doll fit into a child's, a fact that would not be lost on collectors or creators in subsequent years.

Gene's unique face was also controversial. Some in the doll world were quite critical of her blue-grey brows and large eyes, the "whites" of which are actually pale ice blue. However, one must keep in mind that many fashion doll favorites of the past are very stylized as well. A vintage *Barbie®* doll, for example, is much more a creature of fantasy than reality with her tiny, turned-up nose and molded eyelashes. And vintage *Cissy,* to whom Odom credits the inspiration of *Gene's* pensive mouth, is extremely stylized with sleep eyes and childlike proportions combined with a sophisticated wardrobe fit for a debutante. Indeed, to best appreciate *Gene's* face, one must look at her in a black-and-white photograph. Just as many 1940s and 1950s actresses appeared softer and lovelier in the black-and-white films of the day, so too does *Gene*. Her large, startling, icy blue eyes become dreamy, perfectly framed by those blue-grey brows.

The unchanging nature of *Gene's* face paint also sparked controversy. However, that consistency in *Gene's* face is essential to what makes her a special, unique doll. With a change of costume or hairstyle, *Gene* can assume a variety of roles, from ingenue to Egyptian princess to sophisticated chanteuse. Yet, because her face remains the same, she is always *Gene,* no matter what character she is portraying. That face paint is *Gene's* hallmark and an integral part of her magic.

Several months after her debut, the first article about *Gene* in a mainstream doll magazine appeared in the August 1995 issue of *Doll Reader*. For some collectors, this article was a revelation that there were indeed collectible fashion dolls beyond *Barbie®* dolls. "*Gene* was the first fashion doll I collected other than *Barbie®* (dolls)," recalls collector Adele Stitsworth, proprietor of Adele's Fashion Dolls in Pennsylvania. "I absolutely flipped when I first saw her picture in *Doll Reader.* The next month, I saw an ad for *Gene* in *Contemporary Doll Collector* and ordered everything." However, Stitsworth had reservations about this radically different new doll. "At first I was intimidated by her size because I was so used to the 11-½-inch dolls. But I was impressed with *Gene's* style and beauty, with the quality of her fashions and the whole concept of the doll."

However, it took a 1996 article in *Barbie® Bazaar* to get many die-hard *Barbie®* doll collectors to even consider buying *Gene*. Karen Caviale and Marlene Mura have always been progressive in their approach to collectible fashion dolls, frequently featuring articles about the *Barbie®* doll's predecessors and competitors from the 1950s and 1960s as well as cutting-edge contemporary dolls. By publishing an article written by Laura Meisner, featuring photographs by Meisner and Doug James, Mura and Caviale helped not only to promote and introduce *Gene* to the *Barbie®* doll collector community but also to validate her as a legitimate and acceptable collectible. Meisner's eloquent, poetic prose combined with *Gene's* life-like, tastefully sensuous poses in the photos made such an indelible impression on the hearts of many collectors that they were willing to give this doll, so radically different from their beloved *Barbie®* doll, a second chance.

After a rather slow start, *Gene's* popularity took off like wildfire. Articles appeared about *Gene* in mainstream doll and collectibles magazines and *Gene* frequently graced many a magazine cover. One such article appeared in the July 1996 issue of *White's Guide to Collecting Figures*. A stunningly ethereal *Blue Goddess,* flanked by a set of golden wings, appeared on that issue's cover with the irresistible teaser, "Will *Gene* become the next *Barbie®*?" To be sure, collectors who had earlier dismissed *Gene* scrambled to join the *Gene* phenomenon and amass earlier special editions and retired outfits and dolls. With a satisfied twinkle in her voice, Stitsworth remembers the change of heart experienced by many of the members of her local *Barbie®* doll collectors' club. "When the club would meet at my house, I'd have my *Genes* on display and the other club members would tell me that I was wasting my money buying that doll. Of course, now almost all of them collect *Gene* and most of them buy from me!" Additionally, the first retirement of a doll, *Premiere*, piqued the interest of enthusiasts who didn't want to miss out on what could become a valuable collectible. This convinced many collectors of *Gene's* importance as a fashion doll, and secondary market prices for *Premiere* soared in the months following her retirement.

Opposite Page: The first *Gene* to retire was *Premiere*, issued in 1995 and retired in 1997. *Photo courtesy Ashton-Drake.*

One of the most popular *Gene* dolls was *Blue Goddess,* issued in 1996 and retired in 1999. *Photo courtesy Ashton-Drake.*

White Hyacinth Gene was issued in 1997 and retired in 1998. *Photo courtesy Ashton-Drake.*

Left: *Magic-Cloth* dolls representing *Gene* in three different hair colors, with a variety of ensembles. This one is *Blue Goddess* dressed in *Blossoms in the Snow.*

Below: *On the Avenue Gene* was an exclusive for FAO Schwarz in 1998. *Photo courtesy Ashton-Drake.*

Opposite Page: The exquisite *Iced Coffee Gene* was issued in 1997 and retired in 1999. *Photo courtesy of Ashton-Drake.*

A revolutionary in high heels, Ashton-Drake's *Gene* changed the course of fashion doll history forever. *USO Gene*, 1999. *Photo courtesy of Ashton-Drake.*

Five years after the introduction of *Gene*, the doll has evolved into a legend, winning awards and acclaim from all sectors of the collecting community. Moreover, *Gene,* the revolutionary in high heels, has inspired an entire new genre of collectible fashion dolls aimed at adults. But why was *Gene* so successful when other large fashion dolls,

such as Takara's lovely *Lady Luminous*, were not? The answers are multifold.

To begin with, not only was *Gene* a high quality doll, she was user-friendly. Her packaging was such that she had to be removed from her box in order to be displayed. Furthermore, she could be put back into that box without any significant loss of value. Thus, many collectors began to experience *Gene* in a way they could not enjoy *Barbie®* dolls; free from the NRFB mindset, they were able to play with *Gene* without guilt or fear of devaluing the doll. Moreover, *Gene's* larger size facilitated play. It was easier to sew for her, to repaint her, to simply redress her, and collectors who had previously been intimidated by her size grew to appreciate and prefer it.

Gene was also affordably priced. Each of the first five dolls retailed for $69.95 and the price of the initial outfits was $29.95. By the mid-1990s, the cost of vintage *Barbie®* dolls had escalated, pricing many desirable dolls and items out of the reach of many collectors. However, *Gene* became a viable alternative for those collectors. A high quality, finely designed doll with a fabulous wardrobe and oodles of irresistible accessories, she offered many of the same things that were so appealing about vintage *Barbie®* dolls but with a more reasonable price tag. Additionally, *Gene* was priced competitively with contemporary collectible *Barbie®* dolls. Both on the retail and secondary markets, the price of some collector edition *Barbie®* dolls had soared almost as dramatically as had the value of vintage items. Dolls such as the elusive *Gold Jubilee Barbie®*, priced at around $300 retail, were commanding price tags of $1,000 or more shortly after their original issue. And in 1996, Mattel issued the controversial *Pink Splendor Barbie®*, a limited edition collectible that carried a hefty suggested retail price of $900. Many collectors who were frustrated at these high prices on both the retail and secondary markets turned to *Gene.*

Additionally, *Gene* had an appealing, irresistible story line. A sweet but plucky small town girl who made it big in Hollywood, she epitomized the American Dream. Additionally, *Gene* embodied the glamour and the poignancy of the 1940s and 1950s, a time period that is romanticized by many. The popularity of vintage films, the resurrection of swing dancing and big bands and the success of contemporary movies set during World War II such as *Saving Private Ryan* are evidence that the 1940s in particular have a special appeal to the hearts and imaginations of people today. Surely Odom's choice of this time period could not have been better.

Another stroke of brilliance was making *Gene* a believable but decisively fictional character with a strong, carefully laid out "life" story. Although *Gene* is a tribute to the movie actresses Odom loved since childhood, she is not based upon any one real person. Her "life" was thus free of the scandal, tragedy and heartbreak that befell far too many of the cinematic idols of that time. "Most actresses did not have very happy lives and I gave *Gene* the sort of happy ending I would wish upon

This promotional button from 1999 shows three *Simply Gene* dolls, the first ones to sport bendable legs.

any actress I admired," states Odom. Moreover, Odom imbued the character of *Gene* with very specific traits. She is optimistic, multi-talented, tenacious and tough but still very sweet. An impossible persona for a real human, perhaps, but it works perfectly for a character of fiction.

Perhaps, though, the most essential key to *Gene's* phenomenal success is love. *Gene* is surrounded by an aura of sentimentality and unabashed affection that would not be out of place in any Frank Capra film. Odom clearly wears his heart on his sleeve where *Gene* is concerned. At doll signings and chance meetings, he is regaled with collectors' stories of how they play with *Gene,* of how she reminds them of this actress or that, of how *Gene* resembles a relative, a loved one or even themselves. Without a doubt, Odom has heard such stories numerous times; yet he gives each collector the courtesy of his undivided attention and makes each of *Gene's* fans feel truly special. At times, his eyes become misty when a collector divulges an especially poignant tale. Odom's enthusiasm and love for *Gene* is infectious, spread not only to collectors but also to the corporate entities who normally are sequestered behind the scenes. At collector events, it is not uncommon to see Ashton-Drake managers and executives having genuine fun while playing trivia games or swing dancing with the rest of the crowd. It is clear to all that the people behind *Gene* are working hard but they are also having fun. To the jaded observer, it perhaps sounds corny, but it is true; there really is a lot of love in this project. And it is with love that collectors all over the world can share the dream.

Chapter Five

A Revolution Gains Momentum

The mid-90s saw the emergence of fashion dolls that differed not only from *Barbie*® dolls but from *Gene* as well. The popularity of dolls such as Tonner's *American Models*, introduced the year prior to *Gene's* debut, and Madame Alexander's revamped and revitalized *Cissy,* introduced a year after *Gene,* indelibly influenced the standard by which the new genre of collectible fashion dolls would be judged. Unique in size, style and shape, these and other dolls ensured that diversity, rather than conformity, would be the norm for the hobby. Keep in mind that the standard for play line fashion dolls, set by the *Barbie*®, doll was rigid, and any doll that differed from *Barbie*® dolls was doomed to failure. It is because of trend-setting dolls like the *Models* and *Cissy* as well as *Coco, Jackie, Julia* and the dolls of The Franklin Mint that adult collectors can enjoy so many options. Later in this chapter, we'll take a look at the *Hayley,* considered to be the first "knock-off" of *Gene* and examine why her tenure on the market was so short.

Introduced in 1994, the *American Models* were changed slightly in subsequent years. Previously identified only by the outfits in which they were sold, in 1995 the regular line *Models* were given women's names like *Chloe* or *Paige.* The separately-sold fashions were discontinued in 1995, and the year also saw the introduction of *Shonda,* the first African-American *Model.* The edition numbers remained quite limited; in 1995, about 500 of each doll was made. That number increased to 750 in 1996 and 1997 but reverted to 500 in 1998 and 1999.

Something that makes collecting Tonner's *Models* an enjoyable challenge is hunting down the special editions the artist has created for various events and shops. In 1994, *Sydney,* a cool blonde in a short, gold lamé party dress, was produced in a limited edition of 100 for the Dolly Dears convention. Other limited editions were produced for events such as Doll & Teddy Bear Expo East and West and the annual Collectors' United gathering. Special editions were also created for specific retailers. FAO Schwarz has had several exclusives, such as a redheaded version of the 1996 brunette *Vivian* and a spectacular showgirl made for the 1997 opening of the FAO store in Las Vegas. Several independent shops have also had their own exclusives, such as *Ariella,* an ethereal angel done, quite befittingly, for The Angel Keeper Shop.

Tonner further expanded collectors' horizons with the debut of the first male fashion doll, *Eric.* A 21-inch fellow introduced in

The tempestuous heroine *Scarlett O'Hara* makes her debut as a vinyl fashion doll from The Franklin Mint. *Photo courtesy of The Franklin Mint.*

1999, dark-haired *Eric* was the perfect groom for that year's *Felicity* bride. A blonde *Prince Charming,* a limited edition of 50 dolls, was produced in 1999 for the Philadelphia shop Happily Ever After.

Two years after the introduction of the *American Models, Cissy,* the first modern fashion doll, "came home." The updated, upscale new version of *Cissy,* designed by a brilliant team led by the late John Puzewski, dazzled the doll world with her debut in 1996. Clearly this was not the same *Cissy* as the demure, winsome versions that graced the early 1990s. The revamped, revitalized

Cissy had attitude! Although she retained the same face mold as all her predecessors, the new *Cissy* had a signature style all her own, with rich red hair and deep brown sleep-eyes. Designer Mathu Anderson gave *Cissy* extravagant hairstyles and dramatic facial screening; the doll had fuller lips, stronger brows, elaborate eye makeup and a small beauty mark under her left eye. Contemporary *Cissy* was also given a new body. Her jointed legs were the same as original, but her torso was longer with a narrower, articulated waist. Her neck was longer and her figure was made more voluptuous with a larger bosom. This beautiful new body was certainly proportionate with *Cissy's* overscale head and was the perfect medium on which to drape lavish designer clothes and oodles of opulent jewelry.

Another groundbreaking step in the evolution of contemporary *Cissy* was the introduction of an African-American version. Although the Alexander Doll Company had always been progressive in manufacturing and marketing African-American dolls such as *Leslie,* who debuted in 1965, this was the first time that *Cissy* appeared as an ethnic character. In part because of her beauty and in part because she was often hard to find, the African-American *Cissy* proved to be very desirable to collectors, often commanding a higher price on the secondary market than her Caucasian counterpart.

Puzewski, a former designer working with Halston, Carolina Herrera, Arnold Scaasi and Byron Lars, was dedicated to the drama of *Cissy.* Because she was large, 21 inches tall, and had a stylized, overscale head, she could be decked out in elaborate costumes and jewelry that would easily overwhelm smaller dolls. It was that whimsical, "doll-like" appearance that allowed *Cissy* to carry off outrageous, even outlandish designs that might be a little over the edge for real people. The 1996 collection, based on a gemstone theme, featured ensembles that boldly combined patterns; the *Ebony and Ivory Houndstooth*

Michelle was a limited edition *American Model* created for the 1997 Doll and Teddy Bear Expo West by the Robert Tonner Doll Company.

Opposite Page: *Eric* was the first male in the *American Model Collection. Photo courtesy of the Robert Tonner Doll Company.*

Prototype *Cissys* debuted in 1999. Of these, twelve were mass-produced for the public. The dolls that were produced in protype or extremely limited form are denoted. **Front row, left to right:** Madame Alexander in-house design team, Marc Bouwer, Fernando Sanchez and Ellen Tracy. **Middle row, left to right:** Badgley Mischka, Donna Karan (prototype only), Carolina Herrera, Anna Sui, Mary McFadden (prototype only), Josie Natori, Lilly Pulitzer (limited edition of 30 for 1999 Alexander Doll Club Convention), Carmen Marc Valvo (prototype only) and Arnold Scaasi (exclusive to Danbury Mint). **Back row, left to right:** James Purcell, Isaac Mizrahi (prototype only), Dana Buchman, Diane Von Frustenberg (prototype only), Betsey Johnson (prototype only), Yeohlee (prototype only), Nicole Miller (prototype only) and Jessica McClintock. *Photo courtesy of Sally Fischer Public Relations and the Alexander Doll Company.*

Ebony and Ivory Cissy, manufactured by the Alexander Doll Company in 1996.

Suit, for example, matched two different hound-stooth patterns with a striped blouse, grey faux fur hat and stole, and "snakeskin" pumps and a purse. On a smaller fashion doll or on a person, such an ensemble might not work, but on *Cissy,* it's incredible! This was the start of *MA Couture,* a happy marriage of fashion, fantasy and sheer fun.

The 1997 and 1998 offerings pushed the envelope as well. The 1997 *Cissy* line had a flower theme, with dolls dressed in the *Tea Rose Cocktail Ensemble* or the *Calla Lily Evening Column and Bolero.* Also in 1997 the elaborate *Cissy's Secret Armoire* set was introduced.

A sumptuous *Cissy* dressed in a peach teddy came with several exquisite lingerie ensembles and accoutrements for an upscale lady of leisure, all packed in a silk-covered trunk. In 1998, *Cissy* went on a grand tour of Europe via the *Orient Express* and appeared as *Cissy Paris, Cissy Budapest* and two versions, Caucasian and African-American, of *Cissy Barcelona.* The *Orient Express Cissys* were very detailed, very over-the-top and very expensive.

Significant changes to contemporary *Cissy* came in 1999, with a line larger and more diverse than ever. In conjunction with the Council of Fashion Designers of America (CFDA), 20 icons of American style, from Badgley Mischka to Diane Von Furstenberg, were tapped to design ensembles for *Cissy.* The in-house Alexander team created an additional design reminiscent of *Cissy's* past, an understated beauty with an upswept hairstyle and a pink and black mermaid-style gown. The 21 prototypes were slated to be auctioned, with the proceeds benefiting Fashion Targets Breast Cancer (FTBC), which was founded by the CFDA to raise funds for the Nina Hyde Center for Breast Cancer Research at Georgetown University. Of these, variously limited editions of 12 designs were put into mass-production, with part of the proceeds donated to FTBC. Each designer was at liberty to give *Cissy* exactly the look he or she wanted. Thus, some versions had dramatic makeup while others were understated. And while some sported the red hair that had become *Cissy's* signature, others were blonde, brunette, platinum and even pink. The fashions ranged from the post-punk look of the Betsey Johnson to the Nordic-inspired Anna Sui to the conservative and street savvy Linda Allard for Ellen Tracy. Many collectors, accustomed to *Cissy's* opulent and outrageous appearance in previous years were pleasantly surprised at how much they liked some of the simpler, more realistic designs as well.

Sadly, 1999 also brought the untimely death of John Puzewski after a long illness. Fortunately, Puzewski's legacy lives on. Without his foresight and courage to update an icon of the 1950s into the present day, contemporary *Cissy* may not have evolved into the fabulous collectible she is now. Today, *Cissy* is truly stronger and more wonderful than ever, bringing joy to thousands of collectors worldwide. And all indications are that *Cissy* will remain one of the most important collectible fashion dolls for many years yet to come.

No doubt spurred by the success of *Cissy* in 1996, Alexander Dolls introduced a smaller but similar doll the following year. Marketed as "*Cissy's* younger cousin," *Coco* was an adorable, 16-inch blue-eyed blonde made from the original *Elise* face mold. The initial *Coco* offering consisted of a travel ensemble that could be purchased as a set or separately. The set included three outfits: a pink felt suit with luxurious faux fur, a frilly cocktail dress and evening coat and casual capri pants and a sweater set for sightseeing. *Coco* also came with a fuzzy white beanbag dog, *Cleo.* Collectors were delighted with the wonderful hairpieces that came with each ensemble and many began playing with their dolls' hair for the first time. In 1998, *Coco* was a bit less elaborate. *Belle Epoch Coco* consisted of just the doll and two outfits; the dog and hairpieces were not carried over from the previous year.

Right: The 1998 *Cissy* line was the most elaborate and expensive of the company's offerings to date. *Cissy* traveled through Europe on the Orient Express, lavishly dressed in sumptuous outfits and dripping with jewelry. *Budapest Cissy* was a favorite of many collectors that year.

Pearl Bride Cissy, limited to 1,000 dolls, was the most elaborate and most expensive offering of the 1996 line.

Unfortunately, *Coco's* tenure was brief. Legal entanglements over the name *Coco* meant that the doll would be left without a real name in 1999. In her place was a nameless blonde-haired blue-eyed doll dressed in a splendid *Riviera Night* ensemble. *Riviera Day,* a coordinating swimsuit, was sold separately. In addition, other 16-inch dolls made with the *Elise* face were released that year, such as the *Classic Bride.*

In 1997, Madame Alexander brought out yet another fashion doll, *Jackie,* an updated version of a 1961-1962 portrait doll based on the beloved First Lady Jacqueline Kennedy. As with *Cissy, Jackie* sported the original face sculpt combined with updated facial screening and the new, more voluptuous body. Puzewski kept his designs in character with the real Jacqueline, with chic yet conservative ensembles reminiscent of early 1960s haute couture. *Jackie's Travel Collection* consisted of a pink and white evening gown with matching coat, a white and blue cocktail dress, a pink two-piece suit and coordinating jewelry and accessories. Three pieces of luggage came with the set as well. Limited to 2,500 dolls, the set was available only in 1997.

A vinyl fashion doll based on the late Jacqueline Kennedy Onassis became the standard-bearer for a whole new line of designs put out by The Franklin Mint. Already well-known in the doll collecting community as a manufacturer of, among other things, incredibly lifelike porcelain celebrity dolls, The Franklin Mint ventured into vinyl in 1996 with an unbelievable likeness of the beloved First Lady. Standing a little more than 15 inches tall, *Jackie* was an affordably priced, high quality doll with a realistic, well-made wardrobe officially sanctioned by designer Oleg Cassini. *Jackie* was available only via direct response marketing or through The Franklin Mint's stores. The initial issue of *Jackie* was sold separately, with the option open to buyers to get a subscription entitling them to buy her fashions and trunk upon their release. Now, however, *Jackie* has been available for several years and it is possible to purchase whatever fashions are available for her all at once.

With the overwhelming success of *Jackie,* other vinyl versions of popular porcelain portrait dolls were issued. *Marilyn Monroe,* with a wardrobe full of her most famous movie costumes, and *Princess Diana* were released late in the 1990s. Subsequently, vinyl fashion dolls based on fictional characters such as *Scarlett O' Hara, Josephine the Original Gibson Girl* and *Rose DeWitt Bukater,* the romantic protagonist in James Cameron's epic *Titanic.* In addition, several special issues of existing dolls have been released. In 1999, *Happy Birthday Mr. President,* complete with a stand that plays a remastered excerpt of

Monroe's actual performance, was released. Another special edition released in 1999 was *Marilyn Entertaining the Troops,* an edition limited to 5,000 pieces. This specially costumed and wigged doll commemorated Monroe's 1954 goodwill tour in Korea.. Small limited editions have been released as well. An edition of only 25 pieces sold exclusively at the 1999 Doll & Teddy Bear Expo East, *Jackie* wore a recreation of a pink suit worn on Valentine's Day shortly after her husband's inauguration.

The Franklin Mint's fashion dolls are uncannily realistic. The facial sculpting is superb with each doll having a unique face mold. *Jackie* truly looks like the First Lady, *Diana* perfectly resembles the Princess and *Marilyn* is accurate down to her round little nose. Additionally, *Scarlett* and *Rose* are precise depictions of Vivian Leigh and Kate Winslet, the actresses who brought these characters to cinematic life. More amazingly, each doll also has her own body sculpt. *Marilyn* is more curvaceous than *Diana,* who is more athletic in build than *Jackie,* who actually has somewhat large feet. And Kate Winslet's luscious, zaftig figure and glorious, gorgeous face are perfectly replicated in *Rose.*

What's the next vinyl fashion doll for The Mint? A glimpse at their current porcelain offerings might hold a clue. Many collectors fervently hope that a vinyl doll based on *Grace Kelly* will be issued, and one can only wonder if someday a doll based on legendary entertainer *Frank Sinatra* will appear.

Another fashion doll based on a fictional character was *Julia.* Created for the Georgetown Collection by Robert Tonner, *Julia* represented a unique concept in collectible fashion dolls for adults. While for years there have been children's dolls sold with accompanying books, such as Pleasant Company's *American Girls* and Tonner's *Magic Attic Club* (also created for Georgetown), *Julia* was the first fashion doll for adults to be packaged with her own book. *Julia's* book was a romance novel, the story of a beautiful young woman and the mysterious stranger she was to wed. To be sure, the story seemed a little tame as far as romance novels are concerned. Still, there was the requisite, satisfying happy ending and the introduction of new characters around whom subsequent novels could revolve.

Julia, a high quality, seamless, all-vinyl doll who stood a little more than 15 inches tall, was one of the most beautiful fashion dolls of the late 1990s. Her face was one of the most stunning ever sculpted by Tonner, with an aristocratic nose and wonderfully high cheekbones. Her face paint was inherently romantic, with mysterious, heavy-lidded blue eyes and full, rosy lips, and her body was

Right: *Miss St. John* was a limited edition *Cissy* in a suit by Marie Gray, designer of the fabulous *St. John* clothing line. Produced in 1998, only 750 dolls were made and all were marketed exclusively at Neiman Marcus.

Tea Rose Cissy in a hauntingly beautiful African-American version. 1997.

equally beautiful. Proportionate and realistic, *Julia* had womanly hips, slender yet shapely legs and a graceful décolletage. *Julia* was articulated at the waist but had straight legs.

Unfortunately, *Julia* was not the market success she deserved to be. Many collectors could not relate to her romance novel theme and others simply overlooked her. Due to the sale of Georgetown Collection to Ashton-Drake, the fate of *Julia* is uncertain at the time of this writing. It is hoped that *Julia* will not disappear into oblivion, for interest in this vastly underrated doll is rising due to the popularity of Tonner's similarly sized *Tyler Wentworth*.

Near the end of 1998, a doll briefly sold in selected Toys "R" Us stores caused quite the uproar among *Gene* collectors. *Hayley* was a 15-inch vinyl and hard plastic fashion doll made by Soft Luv Doll Ltd., a Hong Kong company that manufactured many exclusive dolls for Toys "R" Us. The first *Gene* "knock-off" or clone, *Hayley* was similar to *Gene* in size and proportion, in appearance and presentation. Her head, like *Gene's,* was slightly overscale and on a reverse socket swivel joint that permitted the same range of motion. *Hayley's* arms and legs were jointed exactly like *Gene's*, and her clavicle and breasts were detailed almost identically to *Gene's*.

There were, however, some slight physical differences between *Hayley* and *Gene* that were readily apparent to the savvy adult enthusiast. *Hayley's* facial sculpting was somewhat more angular, with a narrower, sharper chin, longer nose and more defined jawbone. Her mouth was sculpted with a small gap between her lips so that she could have painted-on teeth. *Hayley* had thicker ankles and calves and her fingers were separated differently. Interestingly, *Hayley* had a twist waist, which *Gene* did not. The material from which *Hayley* was made and her construction were inferior. The plastic was shiny, not matte, and while *Gene* was practically seamless, *Hayley* sported prominent seams on her arms. Many collectors reported that their *Hayley* dolls broke easily, particularly at the waist.

Other differences between the dolls were in the facial painting and the style and quality of the costumes. In contrast to *Gene's* signature look of ice blue eyes and deep bluish-grey brows, *Hayley* came with some variety of eye and eyebrow colors. She had short, painted eyelashes and some versions had painted teeth. *Hayley's* wardrobe was perhaps not the most tastefully designed, nor made with the finest of fabrics. Some of her ensembles were patent "leather" and others consisted of faux fur, leopard prints or corduroy. Some garments were fastened with *Velcro* rather than snaps or hooks and eyes. However, the construction and fit of the garments were good, especially the slacks,

which had pockets and faux fly fronts. Many of *Hayley's* clothes were lined. Her shoes had practically the same construction and base as *Gene's*, although they were made of different materials.

Hayley's packaging and presentation were nearly identical to *Gene's*. The box shape, construction and lining were the same, although *Hayley's* box was decorated with an allover pattern of the script initial "H" and showed a picture of the enclosed doll on the end flap. *Hayley* wore a tag on her left wrist, just like *Gene*. Her stand, clear plastic on a black base with her name embossed in silver, differed from *Gene's* only in the smallest details. *Hayley* was displayed in glass cases in the general doll aisles of the Toys "R" Us stores in which she appeared, perhaps causing some consumers to assume she was a high quality collector edition doll, maybe even *Gene* herself.

Of course, *Hayley* also differed from *Gene* in price. The five dolls sold in casual slacks or day dresses retailed at $29.99 each while the three in formal gowns were $39.99 apiece.

Alarmed at the appearance of this apparent *Gene* clone, Ashton-Drake and Mel Odom filed suit to stop the sale and distribution of *Hayley* and all dolls were subsequently removed from Toys "R" Us shelves. As a result of this legal action, there will be no more *Hayley* dolls manufactured.

Hayley was a controversial figure in the fashion doll world. Some collectors welcomed her as another interesting fashion doll to collect, a "friend" perhaps, for *Gene* and some saw her as the perfect palette for customizing, a less expensive alternative to *Gene* for the collector who merely wanted a doll to repaint or reroot. Others were turned off by the doll's lack of quality and the fact that she was a clone of an existing doll, not something unique or special on her own. And still others saw *Hayley* as a piece of fashion doll history and rushed out to amass as many as possible in order to re-sell. Immediately after the doll was withdrawn from retail, *Hayley* commanded an impressive secondary market price, often up to $200. However, now resale prices have stabilized to around $100 or even less. *Hayley* is a fascinating footnote in the history of contemporary fashion dolls.

But even had *Hayley* not been withdrawn from the market, it is likely that she might not have stayed for long. Just around the corner were some new entries in the fashion doll field that would energize and electrify the entire hobby.

Opposite Page: *Cissy,* in an outfit designed by James Purcell, championed the need for breast cancer awareness and research in 1999. The target motif of her gown is the symbol of Fashion Targets Breast Cancer, and her slip is embroidered with the words: *CFDA Foundation Fashion Targets Breast Cancer 1999. Photo courtesy of Sally Fischer Public Relations and the Alexander Doll Company.*

Arnold Scaasi was tapped again to design for *Cissy* as part of the 1999 line. This stunning blue-eyed redhead was an exclusive sold through the Danbury Mint.

Marketed as the younger cousin of *Cissy, Coco* was issued by the Alexander Doll Company late in 1997.

All of the *Alexander Celebrates American Design Cissy* dolls sported this special hangtag denoting their connection to the Council of Fashion Designers of America's Fashion Targets Breast Cancer.

Each *Julia* doll was accompanied by this romance novel.

Below: *Julia*, created by Robert Tonner for The Georgetown Collection, debuted in 1998.

THE KINGSTON CHRONICLES

Julia

BY PATRICIA MALONE

Opposite Page: This stunning portrait doll of the late *Jacqueline Kennedy Onassis* during her years in the White House, was created by The Franklin Mint. *Photo courtesy of The Franklin Mint.*

72

Marilyn Monroe was another popular vinyl portrait doll for The Franklin Mint. *Photo courtesy of The Franklin Mint.*

Opposite Page: Franklin Mint's *Titanic Rose* is a stunning likeness of actress Kate Winslet and a welcome addition to the company's line of fashion dolls depicting real and fictional heroines. *Photo courtesy of The Franklin Mint.*

Hayley appeared on shelves of select Toys "R" Us stores in late 1998.

Similar yet slightly different. Notice *Hayley's* open mouth and the resemblance of her packaging to *Gene's. From the collection of Barbara "Bops" Blazer.*

Chapter Six

The Year of the Fashion Doll

The year 1999 was pivotal in the fashion doll hobby. The *Gene* line was larger and more popular than ever before; among its highlights were a poignant new USO theme and the introduction of a less expensive, bendable leg *Simply Gene*. Robert Tonner was breaking new ground with the introduction of the first male character, *Eric,* in his popular *American Models Collection.* And, as dis-

Tyler Wentworth in Fragrance Launch, an ensemble from the 1999 line. Photo courtesy of the Robert Tonner Doll Company.

cussed in the last chapter, *Cissy* wowed collectors with the *Madame Alexander Celebrates American Design*, which raised funds for breast cancer research. However, the doll world was stunned at the surprise debut of not one, not two, but three new fashion doll lines. The entry into the market of Tonner's *Tyler Wentworth*, L. L. Knickerbocker's *Somers & Field* and Effanbee's *Brenda Starr*, all larger sized, user-friendly fashion dolls, was essentially a validation of the new genre of fashion dolls. Clearly, this type of fashion doll marketed toward adult collectors was a genuine trend, not a temporary fad or aberration.

Tyler Wentworth was the talk of Toy Fair 1999, and with good reason. Her Robert Tonner pedigree was clearly an assurance that she would be an aesthetically pleasing, high quality doll in the tradition of Tonner's previous creations. The prototypes at Toy Fair were incredible and enthusiastically received by almost everyone who saw them. And to be sure, the production model did not disappoint.

To put it succinctly, *Tyler* is a beautiful, elegant doll. Her clothes are classic yet contemporary, conservative but chic. The epitome of good taste, *Tyler* has a timeless, "old money" style. Many collectors feel that the blonde version of *Tyler* bears a resemblance to the late Carolyn Bessette Kennedy. However, while *Tyler* has a similar air of refinement and grace, any likeness is coincidental and unintentional. Rather, she was born of Robert Tonner's personal tastes and experiences, not patterned after Kennedy or anyone else.

Indeed, *Tyler's* story bears similarity to Tonner's "life before dolls" as a New York fashion designer. A pre-med student on hiatus in New York City, Tonner serendipitously came across an advertisement for the Parsons School of Design and signed up for a summer session. Because registration for his main interest at the time, fashion illustration, was closed, he began studying fashion design and soon won a scholarship to the school. After he received his Bachelor of Fine Arts degree, he worked for a small design company for several years, leaving to become a head designer with the Bill Blass sportswear line, Blassport. Tonner was with Blass for six years, then left to open his own design company. When the financial backing for his own label fell through, Tonner ended up at Blass again.

During Tonner's career as a fashion designer,

This paper doll of *Signature Style Tyler Wentworth,* drawn by Carolyn Myers Williamson, perfectly captures the grace and tastefulness of this lovely doll.

a friend with a passion for antiques introduced him to the world of dolls. Although antique dolls did not appeal to him, Tonner gravitated toward play dolls such as *Sasha* and *Barbie®* dolls. He began to amass a collection and then became interested in sculpting his own dolls. In his spare time, Tonner created a small number of one-of-a-kind dolls each year. Eventually, a change in ownership at Blass cost him his job. At that point, he decided to pursue dollmaking as a career, and, well, we collectors know the rest of that story.

Similarly, *Tyler Wentworth's* story is equally fraught with coincidence. The *wunderkind* of Seventh Avenue, *Tyler* assumed the helm of the prestigious *House of Wentworth* when her great-aunt *Regina,* the founder of the firm, left to pursue romance with an exotic, younger man. As the *Tyler Wentworth* catalog states, "Although young for the job, *Tyler* quickly showed that she was equal to her new responsibilities. With only a few short seasons of fashion experience, she confidently assumed leadership of the *House of Wentworth* and received rave reviews for her first collection." (One can only speculate as to whether *Tyler* will someday "retire" from the fashion industry to become a doll designer herself!)

Tyler has a strong aesthetic appeal. Her lovely face, while not identical to that of the *American Models* or *Julia,* has that unmistakable Tonner "look" with her small, realistically sized eyes and full lips. Her serious, understated facial screening accurately reflects the aesthetic standards of today. Indeed, with her long, straight hair and minimalist makeup, *Tyler* looks as if she walked off the pages of *Vogue, Harper's Bazaar* or *In Style.* Her head sculpt is true-to-life with a well-shaped, slightly aristocratic nose, firm jaw and a head size in proportion with a real woman's body.

Tyler's body is equally beautiful. As with his *American Models,* Tonner's goal was to interpret into doll form a contemporary female ideal, not a standard from a previous generation. In a brilliant, refreshing move, Tonner made *Tyler* slender yet rounded. Unlike far too many women in the fashion and entertainment industries today, *Tyler* is not skeleton-thin. If *Tyler* were a living person, she would be toned, athletic and healthy. She has strong shoulders, full hips and backside with a small but realistic waist. *Tyler's* modestly sized breasts are high, as if pushed up by one of today's more fashionable bras, and each bears the slightest hint of a nipple. Her arms are long and her hands are large but graceful, a hallmark of Tonner's designs. To the delight of collectors, *Tyler* is also posable, with hinged, articulated knees that permit a perfect 90-degree bend. Perfecting that joint at the knees was a labor of love, for it literally took years for Tonner to develop one that would be fairly unobtrusive yet permit a wide range of motion.

The high quality inherent in the doll extends to her wardrobe as well. Her clothes are finely tailored of fine luxurious fabrics such as cashmere and silk. The fit is flawless. Tonner has taken pains to minimize the possibility of outfits staining the dolls; he has lined most black garments or provided a body stocking. The sleeveless turtleneck sweater from the special edition *Market Week* fashion is stitched on the inside with white thread because black thread is often the culprit in staining.

However, Tonner's quest for excellence with *Tyler Wentworth* has not been without considerable challenge. Late in 1999, customers and retailers alike were frustrated with delays in the shipping of the line. As explained by executive assistant Nancy Shomo, the project got behind schedule because of unforeseen problems with the materials used for *Tyler's* body. Previous dolls made by the Robert Tonner Doll Company had all been made of one material. *Betsy McCall* and the *American Models* are completely made of vinyl; the *Kripplebush Kids*, on the other hand, are composed of hard plastic. However, *Tyler* is the company's first doll made of a combination of vinyl and hard plastic. Among the many unexpected adjustments that had to be made was the allowance for the different percentage of shrinkage between the different materials. Hence, the manufacturing process took longer and *Tyler* fell behind schedule.

After the dolls began shipping, however, another finishing problem was discovered that threatened the entire project as well as Tonner's reputation as a manufacturer of high quality dolls. Tonner had originally intended the hair on *Signature Style Tyler* to be parted down the middle. Although the doll wore her hair in a high ponytail, the concept was that the collector had the flexibility to take down the hair if he or she chose to do so. To his dismay, the very first *Signature Style* dolls that shipped had unparted hair. In a letter written to retailers, Tonner explained his dilemma: either he could ship what he felt were dolls of less than the quality he expected or he could delay the shipment and send the dolls back to China so the problem could be corrected. This was a major gamble on Tonner's part. On the one hand, shipping the product immediately to satisfy consumer demand meant that he would risk the ire of those

A *Little Night Music* was an exclusive *Tyler Wentworth* doll sold by Corbett's Collectables in 1999. The edition was limited to 1,000 pieces.

who might feel that *Tyler* was not of the highest quality as she could be. On the other, Tonner was well aware that some collectors and retailers were disappointed that the dolls were shipping behind schedule and he did not wish to frustrate them further by delaying the dolls even more. His reputation was clearly at stake; the doll world is small and if *Tyler* did not meet consumer expectations, the word would spread quickly. It was no small act of courage for Tonner to send the dolls back to the factory to get *Tyler* perfect. Indeed, this action infuriated some, but for most, all was forgiven when their *Tyler* orders arrived. Most collectors agreed that she was well worth the wait and many began pre-ordering the 2000 line even before Toy Fair.

Robert Tonner is constantly striving to improve the doll he considers to be among his finest work. He, like Mel Odom, is a fashion doll collector, acutely aware of adult tastes and preferences. Moreover, Tonner is a perfectionist, always seeking excellence in the dolls he creates. For example, he made subtle changes that differentiate the first issues of *Signature Style Tyler* from all subsequent production runs. The first *Signature Style* dolls to reach consumers had unpainted scalps and very understated makeup but later production runs have painted scalps and slightly more vivid facial screening.

In an interview for this book, Tonner stated that *Tyler* was not just a progression from his earlier porcelain fashion dolls or even from his *American Models*. Rather, she had been his concept all along, an ideal that took literally years to bring to fruition. Tonner wanted his creation to embody his standards of high quality and high fashion in an affordable, user-friendly doll. It looks like he has succeeded.

If *Tyler Wentworth* is as elegant as a symphony, L. L. Knickerbocker's *Somers & Field* line is as fresh and effervescent as rock 'n' roll. To be specific, *Willow Somers* and *Daisy Field*, two teenage girls living in London in the Swinging Sixties, are as vibrant, exciting and complex as the popular music of that day. Moreover, *Daisy* and *Willow* represent the most unique fashion doll concept of the new genre, and that uniqueness is not limited to the time period on which their creators chose to concentrate.

J. Douglas James and Laura Meisner, the creative masterminds behind *Somers & Field*, have been best friends for over a decade, initially brought together by a mutual passion for dolls. Over the years, the two collaborated on numerous projects, including *Gene*. However, James and Meisner felt a burning desire to make their own statement to the fashion doll world, to contribute something new to a genre that had so enriched their own lives. Thus began their occasionally tumultuous journey as *Willow* and *Daisy* evolved from concept to prototype to finished product.

In an article written for the August/September 1998 issue of *Miller'$ Fashion Doll*, Meisner explained how *The Mod British Birds* came to be. She and James, who had contemplated doing their own fashion doll for some time, were approached by Fiore, a sculptor and mutual friend. Fiore, aware of the friends' interest in creating a doll, showed them a sculpt that was, in Meisner's words, "youthful, charming and realistic without being a wax figure." The sculpt was readily conducive to Meisner and James' vision of a doll based on a teenager in the 1960s, an exciting period in fashion and pop culture that had not been addressed since the heyday of *Twist 'N Turn*

Barbie® and *Francie, Barbie®'s 'MOD'ern Cousin.* Moreover, the shape and size of the head as well as the facial features would readily lend themselves to stylization, giving the dolls the whimsical, delightful, "doll-like" qualities both admired in vintage fashion dolls like *Cissy* and *Jill*.

Meisner and James began carefully researching the styles that epitomized "Youthquake," a term coined in the mid 1960s by *Vogue* editor Diana Vreeland to describe the emphasis on fun, fashion and, most importantly, youth. The colorful, cutting-edge designs of forward-thinkers like Mary Quant, Correges and Paco Rabane energized and inspired them to create miniskirts, bell-shaped dresses with Empire waists and even a vinyl Edwardian suit. The two also meticulously studied the hair and makeup styles of the time to ensure accuracy and congruency with the fashions. Realizing the importance of a strong story to which collectors could identify, Meisner and James chose to place them in Swinging London at the very height of the Mod era. The brilliance of this move cannot be understated. First, London was the epicenter of Youthquake and most of the hottest trends of the day in fashion, beauty and even popular culture were British in origin. Carnaby Street had far more influence in fashion than Seventh Avenue, and the top models of the day, including Twiggy, Jean Shrimpton and Penelope Tree, were British "birds." A second "British invasion" overran the United States, lead by popular musicians such as the Beatles, Petula Clark, Herman's Hermits and the Rolling Stones. Swinging London was happening, baby! In contrast, America was wrestling with several sobering issues that polarized the country. The struggle for civil rights, Vietnam and, later, Watergate color many Americans' memories of those years with a grim sense of seriousness. By placing *Daisy* and *Willow* in London, however, Meisner and James have deftly sidestepped these volatile issues. The dolls are meant to bring back the happier memories of the Mod years, the fashions and the fun, rather than the pain and political divisiveness of that time. With the current popularity of 1960s nostalgia, such as the *Austin Powers* movies, it is apparent that people are able to look back at that period with the positive, enjoyable aspects in mind rather than dwell solely on the serious issues.

Another wonderfully creative twist in the story of *Willow* and *Daisy* was casting them as the daughters of the owners of the most fashionable, albeit fictional, department store in the land, *Somers & Field of London*. This clever move opened the door to an exploration of the myriad

Opposite Page: *Party of the Season Tyler Wentworth* was an edition limited to 2,500 dolls in 1999. *Photo courtesy of the Robert Tonner Doll Company.*

The *Signature Style Tyler* with red hair (left) sports subdued facial screening and does not have a painted scalp, whereas the blonde doll (right), manufactured in a subsequent run, has brighter makeup and a painted scalp.

The original prototypes of *Somers & Field.* Prototype *Daisy Field* (left) is dressed in *Jazz Club* and prototype *Willow Somers* wears the original concept for *Spring Collection. Photo by Steven Mays, courtesy of Doug James & Laura Meisner.*

fashions offered in the line. From haute couture to upscale "hippie chic," *Daisy* and *Willow* have virtually unlimited access to every cutting-edge style available and the freedom to experiment with the looks of the day. Frankly, what self-respecting clotheshorse (or fashion doll collector) could be immune to such a delicious fantasy?

The concept of *Daisy*, the ethnic doll in the pair, was particularly brilliant. James and Meisner wanted to do a doll of color, but did not want her to be merely an afterthought or a supporting player. Hence, they decided that the line should have two lead dolls of equal importance rather than just one main character. Moreover, they gave *Daisy* an exotic British/Hindu heritage. Not only was this an ethnicity not previously explored in the fashion doll world, it also tapped into the vast Indian influence on British popular culture during the Mod years. Aesthetically, the exotic, caramel-colored *Daisy* is a perfect complement to the fair-skinned *Willow*. The dolls display fabulously well together and, even though they share the same face mold, each retains her own unique look and identity. The various ensembles look quite different on each of the dolls, giving the collector a much wider range of options for redressing the dolls.

In many ways, the concept of two lead dolls is a metaphor for the relationship, both personal and professional, between Meisner and James. Just as *Willow* and *Daisy* are best friends on equal standing, so too are their creators. They work exceedingly well together and share a similar vision, although they occasionally take slightly different approaches. James is a veteran costume designer and milliner whose experience ranges from theater to film to television, including longstanding stints with *Saturday Night Live* and the *Muppets*. He has earned wide acclaim in the doll world for the meticulous detail he puts into his designs. His work is painstakingly historically accurate and he almost always adds some small touch to each design that renders it particularly poignant or whimsical. Meisner, a doll restoration expert and widely regarded authority, brings to the partnership impeccable taste and a deep appreciation for fabric drape and texture as well as an innate talent for design. The two complement each other perfectly. Doug James states that nothing in the *Somers & Field* line is strictly the contribution of one partner. "We influence each other and give each other ideas and input. There's a little of Laura in everything I design and a little of me in the things Laura designs." Moreover, as doll collectors themselves, the two possess a keen understanding of the sensibilities of the adult hobbyist. Both are committed to producing dolls and fashions of high quality, well made with the finest materials available, and to doing the best job possible.

With prototype dolls and fashions in hand, a singular vision and a partnership built on deep friendship and mutual respect, James and Meisner set off to bring their shared dream to fruition. The process of finding a corporate home for the project was much swifter than the partners expected. Indeed, shortly after Meisner's article in *Miller'$ Fashion Doll* came out, James and Meisner were in negotiations with the L. L. Knickerbocker company to manufacture and distribute the line.

The prototype *Willow Somers* and *Daisy Field* dolls, painted by renowned fashion doll artist Ken Bartram, took the doll world completely by surprise when they appeared at Knickerbocker's booth at the 1999 Toy Fair. Of course, this was only a sneak peek, for the dolls' official debut was slated to be that June year at the International Collectible Exposition at Rosemont, Illinois. Many Toy Fair attendees were impressed with the line, especially the costuming and facial paint, while others expressed reservations about the awkwardness of the initial sculpt, especially the neck and jawbone. In all fairness, this was just a prototype, and James and Meisner had already planned refinements to the sculpt to make it more graceful.

The necessary refinements were made to the sculpt and dolls from the master molds were shown to an enthusiastic crowd at Rosemont. However, the *Somers & Field* project suffered a number of challenges. One such obstacle was with the articulation of the dolls' bodies. Meisner and James were both fans of *Dollikin,* a multi-jointed fashion doll from the late 1950s, and wanted *Daisy* and *Willow* to be fairly posable as well. They originally intended the dolls to have bendable legs and twist waists. However, with the revealing fashions worn by the dolls, such articulation proved to be aesthetically unsatisfactory and the knee and waist joints were deferred. Another problem was with the dolls' stands. Meisner and James objected to the saddle stands that come with most contemporary fashion dolls because this kind of stand might interfere with the drape of the dolls' costumes, particularly the short skirts and hot pants. A different type of stand could not be perfected in time and the 1999 dolls were shipped without stands.

But something even more ominous overshadowed the project, for the L. L. Knickerbocker Company was in the throes of a financial crisis. Rumors about the company's future and the fate of

Opposite Page: These were the prototypes shown by the L. L. Knickerbocker Company at Toy Fair 1999. While they still have the original sculpting, their face paint has been done by Ken Bartram. The girls are wearing some of the pieces from the *Rock 'N' Roll* ensemble. *Photo by Steven Mays, courtesy of the L. L. Knickerbocker Company.*

Opposite Page: *Daisy Field* holds a special place in the history of collectibles, for she is the first ethnic lead doll in the next generation of fashion dolls. Half-British and half-Hindu, *Daisy* has an exotic, yet innocent appearance that charms many collectors. This prototype is dressed in the *Piccadilly* ensemble. *Photo by Steven Mays, courtesy of L. L. Knickerbocker.*

Production model *Willow* in *Jazz Club. From the collection of Aurea Vilar, photo by James & Meisner.*

Production model *Daisy* in *Trafalgar Square. From the collection of Aurea Vilar, photo by James & Meisner.*

87

Comic book heroine *Brenda Starr* was brought back into the fashion doll world in 1999 by the Effanbee company. *Brenda* appeared in three dressed doll incarnations, as a Reporter, in her Starr Gown and in her Penoir. *Photo courtesy of Effanbee and The Zachary Group.*

the line flew over the Internet. People "in the know" insisted that the dolls would never go into production, even though they were being manufactured at that very time! And when the dolls finally shipped, there were new problems. Personnel changes at Knickerbocker hampered the lines of communication and, as a result, mistakes were made with some orders.

However, the struggle to bring the project from prototype to product was worthwhile, for collectors are delighted with *Somers & Field.* Impressed with the beauty, quality and utter charm of these dolls, many collectors have become enthusiastic fans of the line. Moreover, the line is not only unique in addressing a previously overlooked era but also groundbreaking in its use of an ethnic character as one of two lead dolls. Recognition is certainly due James and Meisner for their determination, commitment and creative vision. With the support of the collecting community, *Somers & Field* stands an excellent chance of becoming one of the strongest fashion doll lines in the industry.

Another surprise at Toy Fair 1999 was Effanbee's *Brenda Starr,* the latest doll incarnation of the famed comic strip character. An earlier version, made by the Alexander Doll Company, debuted in 1964 and represented Madame Alexander's attempt to break into the children's fashion doll market. That doll, in spite of her charming sleep eyes and obvious Alexander high quality, was unable to compete with *Barbie®* dolls and thus was not sold for very long. Thirty-five years later, Effanbee resurrected the notion of a fashion doll based on the beloved character, only their interpretation of *Brenda Starr* was the size and scale of *Gene* and the other larger fashion dolls aimed at the adult market.

Brenda Starr debuted on June 29, 1940 in a comic book supplement to the Sunday "funnies" in the *Chicago Tribune. Brenda* was clearly ahead of her time, for, while journalism was an acceptable profession for a woman at that time, most female reporters were relegated to writing the society pages. *Brenda,* on the other hand, had adventures to rival those of her male counterparts, real and fictional. Her creator, too, was ahead of her time. Dalia Messick, who changed her first name to the gender-ambiguous Dale for professional use, was one of the first female cartoonists. This pioneering woman and her equally progressive creation captured the hearts of millions of Americans, elevating *Brenda Starr* from mere cartoon character to cultural icon. *Brenda* also caught the fancy of the entertainment industry, and throughout the years, numerous *Brenda Starr* movies and television projects have been made.

Effanbee tapped renowned doll artist Sandra Bilotto to transform the two-dimensional *Brenda*

Stepping Out Brenda Starr, which sported a sterling silver and diamond pendant, was limited to 1,000 dolls in 1999. *Photo courtesy of Effanbee and The Zachary Group.*

to her present fashion doll form. A strung, vinyl doll, *Brenda* has a beautifully detailed body sculpt, complete with ribcage, navel and clavicle. Her head, a little overscale for her body, is also quite detailed, and when her trademark long red hair is combed just the right way, the doll bears a slight resemblance to actress Brooke Shields, who portrayed *Brenda Starr* in a 1989 movie. Some collectors note a similarity between the overscale head of Brenda Starr and that of Ideal's Tammy from the early 1960s. The proportions are indeed similar and both dolls share a charming, endearing quality that appeals to collectors who appreciate stylized fashion dolls.

Brenda's outfits are based on actual drawings done by Messick for the comic strip. Her ensembles the first year, available only on dressed dolls, included a teal reporter's suit, a pink peignoir, a red and gold *Starr Gown* and a black and fuchsia cocktail gown. The latter, which included a sterling silver star pendant with a real diamond, was a limited edition of only 1,000 pieces.

More of Messick's artwork, as well as the history of *Brenda Starr,* can be found on her packaging. The box is a collector's piece in itself, printed with cartoon drawings of *Brenda* throughout the years. By the way, Effanbee plans to take *Brenda* through the whole range of her fashions since her inception, from the tailored looks of the early 1940s through contemporary styles.

With the introduction of these three groundbreaking lines, *Brenda Starr, Tyler Wentworth* and *Somers & Field,* 1999 was the biggest year to date for the new genre of fashion dolls. But 2000 was to be even bigger.

Chapter Seven

Fashion Dolls of the New Millennium

If 1999 was a pivotal year for the new generation of collectible fashion dolls, 2000 is phenomenal! Innovations and introductions of new characters have invigorated existing lines, and the doll world is abuzz over several new doll lines that debuted at Toy Fair. The category of user-friendly fashion dolls for adult collectors is the fastest growing and most exciting faction of the doll world today, enticing people who never would have imagined themselves as doll collectors and enhancing the lives of those already involved in the hobby.

The year may have marked *Gene's* fifth anniversary, but it was her fans who got all the surprises, the most earth-shattering of which was the introduction of a new character. *Madra Lord*, *Gene's* rival, is perhaps the most brilliant concept in the line since the inception of *Miss Marshall* herself. A gimlet-eyed hellcat with a face reminiscent of Joan Crawford's and an attitude like *Cruella DeVil's*, *Madra* is the perfect foil for the lovely, sweet-natured *Gene*. While *Gene* is classy, cool and obviously grateful for her stardom, *Madra* is scrappy, nasty and ambitious at all costs. The press kit announcing *Madra's* debut summed it up pretty well: "Beauty, Talent and Temper—Watch out for *Madra Lord.*" Oh, and for the record, don't try to soften her name by pronouncing it *"MAHD-rah."* It's *"MAD-rah"* with an emphasis on the *"MAD."*

Madra Lord, Gene's nemesis, was the talk of Toy Fair 2000. *Drawing by Mel Odom, reprinted with permission of Mel Odom and Ashton-Drake.* © 2000 Ashton-Drake Galleries.

Certainly, the reader might be wondering why such an overbearing character as *Madra* is being touted as a brilliant, fabulous addition to the *Gene* line. Mel Odom explains it succinctly. "I didn't want a *Barbie®* (doll) and *Midge* scenario, with one doll and her best friend. These are dolls for adults and conflict is more interesting, more dramatic and more adult." In addition, Odom points out the many real-life rivalries that developed between actresses during the heyday of Hollywood in the 1940s and 1950s, and reasons that it's only logical that *Gene* would acquire a nemesis as well. And what a nemesis *Madra* is! *Madra* is the polar opposite of *Gene*, an "anti-*Gene,*" so to speak. And herein lies the genius. While *Gene* may be a character that people love, *Madra* is one they love to hate. And seriously, who isn't intrigued with the villain, the dastardly scoundrel or the soap opera shrew who finally gets his or her just desserts?

Madra also brings to the *Gene* line a refreshing dollop of humor. Everything from her story line to her wardrobe to the explanation as to why she has stone dogs instead of "real" ones is wickedly peppered with sly, subtle witticisms. She officially missed the annual *Gene* gala for Toy Fair attendees because "she had chipped her nail polish." Her clothes, wonderfully campy and outrageous, have names like *Dressed to Kill*, *Pink With Envy* and *So Evil My Love. Gene* may be *Breathless* but *Madra* is

Opposite Page: *First Encounter Madra. Photo courtesy of Ashton-Drake.*

Heartless. (By the way, she has statues of dogs instead of "live" canines because "REAL dogs shed.")

Although *Gene* probably could raid *Madra's* closet and vice versa, there are a few dissimilarities in their bodies. *Madra* stands ¼ of an inch taller than *Gene* and has a slightly different figure. In addition, she has articulated knees and elbows. *Madra* sports a completely new face mold and her own unique facial screening. In 2000, one open edition redheaded *Madra* doll, sumptuously dressed in *First Encounter,* will be issued, as well as six additional outfits. *Highland Fling* is a costume limited to 3,500 pieces and the raven-haired *Black Widow* will be limited to 2,500 dressed dolls.

Other innovations and fabulous new designs highlight the rest of the *Gene* line. *Twilight Rumba,* a two-piece, lavishly beaded lavender dress designed by Doug James, is the 2000 Annual Edition. Two hundred Artist Proofs, dolls made prior to the actual production of the edition, were sold at FAO Schwarz in New York City at a yearly special event that coincides with Toy Fair. In the regular line, *Gene* stars in new two movies this year, one as a silent screen star who marries into royalty and another as a ranch owner in her first Western. A new *Simply Gene* sports platinum hair and a twist waist. In addition to her other movie costumes and off-screen wear, *Gene* has several accessory packs, including hats and purses and shoes. In addition, her furniture line is expanded.

This year, most dressed *Gene* dolls and outfits are limited to no more than 5000 pieces per edition, with some items limited even further. This move caused controversy among *Gene* collectors and dealers. Some welcomed it because it would bolster demand, especially on the secondary market. Others were displeased because it meant they might miss out on some items, especially if speculation is widespread. This is certainly something to watch, for it will indeed affect the future of *Gene.* And we are all aware that *Gene* is a doll who starts trends rather than follows them.

Tyler Wentworth rang in the millennium with style. Toy Fair attendees were treated to a fabulous fashion show at Robert Tonner's alma mater, the Parsons School of Design, with gorgeous models decked out in people-sized renditions of *Tyler's* various outfits. Regular line dolls and outfits from the premiere collection and the *Spring Collection* were on display, as well as the special editions and the *Fall Collection,* which will debut later this year. A special edition outfit, *Market Week,* was available for purchase at the fashion show. *Tyler* continues her tradition of contemporary class with several dressed dolls and separately sold outfits. *Tyler Wentworth Couture* is limited to 3,000 pieces while the *Tyler Wentworth Prêt*

A Porter ensembles will be open editions. There will be two dressed dolls this spring, as well as the popular *Signature Style* and *Something Sleek, Tyler* dressed in a swimsuit. The dressed dolls are limited to 3,000 each while the basic dolls are open stock.

Moreover, *Tyler's* world expands to welcome a new character, *Esmé,* an African-American premed student turned supermodel. *Esmé* is an exquisite doll, made from the same body mold as *Tyler* but with an ethnically correct face sculpt. Tonner has a true gift in capturing the beauty of the African-American face, and *Esmé* is eagerly anticipated by collectors.

At Toy Fair, Tonner had even more surprises for the fashion doll connoisseur with the debut of *Kitty Collier,* a delightful 18-inch vinyl fashion doll with blue, glass inset eyes. With her winsome face and those hauntingly beautiful yet adorable eyes, *Kitty* looks almost like a grown-up version of Tonner's popular and delightful *Betsy McCall.* She also bears a strong resemblance to Tonner's porcelain *Decades of Fashion* dolls. *Kitty,* with a decidedly 1950s charm, is a dress shop owner "in a make believe time and a fantasy place." She will be sold as a basic doll, with a choice of three hair colors, as well as a dressed doll, with some outfits sold separately.

Two 19-inch vinyl dolls similar to the *American Models,* representing the timeless romantic *heroines Maid Marion* and *Guinevere,* were shown by the Robert Tonner Doll Company at Toy Fair 2000. However, a decision was made after Toy Fair that they would not be produced as part of the 2000 line. For now, the *American Models Collection* is on hold, as focus shifts to *Tyler Wentworth* and *Kitty Collier.*

This may be a new millennium, but the Age of Aquarius is where it's at with the 2000 *Somers & Field* line. This year, two basic dolls in outré swimsuits, wild beach hats and fabulous hairpieces are offered. *Willow* sports a light blonde "boy" cut while *Daisy* has a deep brunette asymmetrical bob, and the coordinating hairpieces fit and blend perfectly. This basic version of *Daisy* sports frosty white lips. Two dressed dolls are also available: *Daisy in Supper With Friends,* a peach-colored chiffon confection with hot pants and thigh high boots, and *Willow in Go-Go Girl,* a futuristic silver minidress reminiscent of the clothes on *Star Trek* or *Barbarella.* The dressed *Willow* has strawberry blonde hair while *Daisy* has deep auburn side ponytails. All four dolls will be limited to one year of production. The separately

Opposite Page: Platinum *Simply Gene* in the ensemble *The Spirit of the Truth. Photo courtesy of Ashton-Drake.*

sold outfits run the gamut from groovy to graceful, including a *Grand Prix Costume* with a purse shaped like a car and a deep blue gown celebrating *Somers & Field 25th Anniversary*, an outfit that will be limited to 1,500 pieces. Two ensembles, *Kings Road* and *At The Captain's Table*, will be limited to 2,800 pieces each while the rest of the fashions will be limited to 2,500 each.

As in 1999, the big event for the *Somers & Field* line will be at the International Collectible Exposition at Rosemont, Illinois, an event that is open not only to the trade but to the public as well. More items will be introduced, including a new character, *Gabrielle Miró*, a French Creole girl the same age as *Willow* and *Daisy*. *Gabrielle* meets the girls on holiday in Paris and, upon discovering that they all are enrolled at the same school in London, the three become fast friends. Because *Gabrielle* is of a mixed French and African-American heritage, she will have features that are decidedly African in nature, not European. She will have a different face mold, one with a broader nose. Her skin color will be a little lighter than *Daisy's*, and she will have grey-blue sideglancing eyes. *Gabrielle's* exotic looks will be further enhanced by her medium reddish brown hair. Initially, *Gabrielle* will be available in a gift set, with a daytime outfit, a cocktail outfit, a coat with hat and gloves, baby doll pajamas, shoes, bedroom scuffs and possibly boots, a piece of luggage and even miniature postcards that she can "send" to her family and friends back home.

Trendy, contemporary teenagers are translated into doll form via a new offering from The Family Company. *Kate,* sculpted by Robert Tonner and issued last year in porcelain, is offered in vinyl, accompanied by two friends, *Melissa* and *Brittany*. *Kate* is a beautiful brunette while *Melissa* is blonde and *Brittany* is African-American. Incidentally, the faces of *Brittany* and *Melissa* were sculpted by well-known artist Sandra Bilotto, and former Mattel designer Carol Spencer created the outfits worn on the three "basic" dolls.

Although the *Kate and Friends* line is similar to many other fashion dolls currently on the market, there are some fascinating differences. First of all, although they are approximately the same height and scale as *Gene, Tyler,* and *Somers & Field,* they sport flat feet! Second, they are truly "bridge" collectibles in that they will have equal appeal to children and collectors alike. They have themes that center on public service and other positive values; their clothing is colorful enough to attract older children and there will be a set of collector cards sold with each doll. However, the dolls are beautiful and sophisticated enough that they will readily appease adult collectors as well. In addition, some of the proceeds from *Kate and Friends* will be donated to *Give Kids The World,* an organization dedicated to realizing the dreams of terminally ill children.

The venerable Alexander Doll Company continues to wow collectors with its sumptuous *Cissy* as well as some tempting new entries in the fashion doll market. This year, *Cissy* travels to the most marvelous cities in the world, from *New York* to *Rome* to *Vienna* to *Singapore*. An exotic *Cissy* with caramel-colored skin, black hair and blue eyes visits *Cairo* while both Caucasian and African-American *Cissys* journey to *Hollywood*. Additionally, a *Romantic Dreams Cissy* will be available as well as an incredible *Scarlett O'Hara Portrait* brilliantly made with the *Cissy* face.

The doll formerly known as *Coco* returns this year with a new name, new persona and presumably a new attitude. *Ivana*, named after the opulent first Mrs. Trump, is a 16-inch blonde with the *Elise* face. She is dressed in an slinky black velvet gown and carries a spider pin. Alexander designer Steve Skutka, a gentleman well known in the fashion doll hobby for breathtakingly beautiful *Barbie®* doll creations, created *Ivana's* ensemble.

The big fashion doll news at Alexander was the introduction of *Alexandra Fairchild Ford*, a 16-inch doll done in the same scale as *Tyler Wentworth* and *Gene*. *Alex* has a beautifully sculpted body and a stylized, somewhat overscale head. To be sure, she has an interesting, delightfully unusual beauty like that of actresses Minnie Driver, Sarah Jessica Parker and Mira Sorvino. In keeping with her unconventional, mercurial nature, *Alex* will sport a variety of hair and eye colors. Her contemporary wardrobe is eclectic, from classic ballgowns to embroidered slacks, with everything from luscious sweaters and belly button jewels in between. Among her designers are Skutka and *Gene* team alumnus Timothy Alberts. *Alex* is depicted as the editor of a small fashion magazine, and her ensembles correlate to that theme. In the 2000 line there are seven dressed dolls, two separately sold outfits and several accessory packs.

Effanbee expands its *Brenda Starr* line in 2000 with several new dressed dolls and separately sold outfits. Two dolls, *Belle of the Ball* and the lovely *Anniversary Gala* honoring the 60th anniversary of the *Brenda Starr* comic, will be limited to 2000 pieces each. The four outfits that are available can be purchased separately or on dressed dolls. Additionally, there is a *Starter Doll* clad in lacy undergarments and a feather boa, and three of the dressed dolls from 1999 are carried over into 2000.

Opposite Page: *Twilight Rumba Gene,* the 2000 Annual Edition Doll. *Photo courtesy of Ashton-Drake.*

A surprise new entry in the fashion doll field was *Eve,* created by doll artist Susan Wakeen, best known for winsome and adorable child and baby dolls. To be sure, this is not Wakeen's first venture into fashionable dolls, for in the past fifteen years she has made several porcelain ladies of fashion. However, the approximately 16-inch tall *Eve* is Wakeen's first vinyl fashion doll. In an article by Mary Graff in the March/April 2000 *DollReader,* Wakeen recalls happy memories of her childhood *Barbie®* doll and her dreams of how she would create a fashion doll if she were a doll designer.

Eve has a special sweetness about her. While her style is contemporary, it is frillier and more romantic than either *Alex* or *Tyler.* Perhaps one could say that while *Tyler* typifies New York, the enchanting *Eve* is Atlanta, Georgia. To be sure, with her fresh, feminine face and expressive eyes, one can easily imagine *Eve* decked out in a Laura Ashley-inspired frock, sipping iced tea under a magnolia tree.

The 2000 line will include several dressed dolls and two basic swimsuit versions. One of these basic dolls will be African-American. There will also be about six additional outfits. It is expected that *Eve* will begin shipping in the autumn of 2000.

Kingstate is another company new to the adult collectible fashion doll market, having introduced their 16-inch fashion doll, *Micki,* at Toy Fair 2000 as well. The *Micki* line is well-conceived and extraordinarily complete, with four characters available as dressed and basic dolls, separately sold ensembles, fabulous accessory packs and even a trunk slated to be released this first year. *Micki,* an exotic brunette with perhaps a Mediterranean or Eurasian air, is the lead doll, with her friends *Maggi,* a green-eyed redhead, *Marni,* a blue-eyed blonde and *Marissa,* a decidedly ethnic doll with rich brown skin, black hair and brown eyes. The first four dolls, dressed in identical outfits, will be limited to 2,500 each. Nominated for *Doll Reader's 2000 DOTY (Doll Of The Year)* award, *Micki* sports facial painting by the talented Holly Miner and contemporary, realistic fashions designed by the gifted Linda Schuck.

One thing in the *Micki* line that fashion doll collectors simply cannot overlook is the incredible shoe pack. The meticulous detailing on the shoes is fabulous and, best of all, the shoes will fit most other 15 to16 inch high heeled fashion dolls.

Also, popular fashion doll lines are to be continued by The Franklin Mint. Because The Franklin Mint sells directly to customers via the Internet, catalog sales and in its own stores, it does not show any dolls at Toy Fair. However, we can expect the continuation and expansion of both the *Scarlett O'Hara* and *Titanic Rose* lines this year,

and more surprises for collectors are surely planned.

But perhaps the biggest surprise of Toy Fair 2000 is something that did not happen. Many fashion doll enthusiasts fully expected Mattel to enter the 15 to 16 inch fashion doll market this year but were surprised when this didn't occur. However, what Mattel did do was introduce a doll with many of the same qualities of the popular new larger fashion dolls but in a *Barbie®*-sized package. The new *Fashion Model Barbie®,* available as either a blonde or brunette, is a fascinating mix of the old and the new. She sports a vintage face but has a contemporary, more realistically proportioned body and classic, yet current wardrobe. Her body is made of a patented new material called *Silkstone* and she is a much heavier doll than current play line or collector edition *Barbie®* dolls. In addition, she is strung rather than socket jointed, a first in the *Barbie®* doll's history. The manufacturing process renders this new doll completely seamless, something sure to please a wide range of collectors.

Certainly, the new *Fashion Model* seems to have far more in common with *Gene, Tyler* or *Somers & Field* than with "traditional" collectible *Barbie®* dolls. Her packaging is user-friendly and she can be put back in the box with ease. Although there is a dressed doll, the *Delphine Barbie®,* in this line, the basic dolls are sold in lingerie, with two separately-sold ensembles available. Robert Best, one of the *Barbie®* doll's most beloved and respected designers, is responsible for the line's design.

What will be the eventual impact of this strategy? Is Mattel making a mistake by not entering the burgeoning market of larger-sized fashion dolls or is the company being extremely wise in sticking with what it does best? Frankly, whether Mattel eventually enters this market or not, the consumer is the ultimate winner. A revised and revamped *Barbie®* doll targeted toward fashion doll connoisseurs is obviously good for the hobby. Todays fashion doll enthusiasts embrace diversity, standards by which the next generation are judged is flexible, not rigid. If it can encompass dolls as large as *Cissy,* why not dolls as small as the *Barbie®* doll as well? And if Mattel would introduce its own 15-1/2-inch fashion doll, the doll would certainly find a niche and attract a following. This is truly fashion doll history evolving in front of our eyes and something that will definitely impact the future of the hobby.

Opposite Page: *Tyler Wentworth* models her *Shakespeare in the Park* ensemble for 2000. *Photo courtesy of the Robert Tonner Doll Company.*

Above: *Esmé*, a beautiful African-American, is the first new character introduced in the *Tyler Wentworth Collection.* *Photo courtesy of the Robert Tonner Doll Company.*

Above: *Kitty Collier* is Robert Tonner's whimsical fashion doll salute to the 1950s. *Photo courtesy of the Robert Tonner Doll Company.*

Left: The *Somers & Field* line introduces a mannequin in 2000, in keeping with their department store theme. *Photo by James & Meisner.*

The Family Company's *Kate*, sculpted by Robert Tonner, is being produced in vinyl in 2000.

Vienna Cissy is another exquisite design in the 2000 line. *Photo courtesy of Sally Fischer Public Relations and the Alexander Doll Company.*

Alexandra Fairchild Ford is the newest fashion doll sensation from the Alexander Doll Company. This trendy version is Museum Gala Alex. Photo courtesy of Sally Fischer Public Relations and the Alexander Doll Company.

Left: *Alex* in her *Editor-in-Chief* ensemble. *Photo courtesy of Sally Fischer Public Relations and the Alexander Doll Company.*

Opposite Page: Effanbee celebrates the 60th anniversary of the *Brenda Starr* comic strip with this elegant *Anniversary Gala* dressed doll. *Photo courtesy Effanbee and The Zachary Group.*

Susan Wakeen enters the fashion doll arena with *Eve*, a lovely doll that embodies contemporary femininity. *Photo courtesy of the Susan Wakeen Doll Company.*

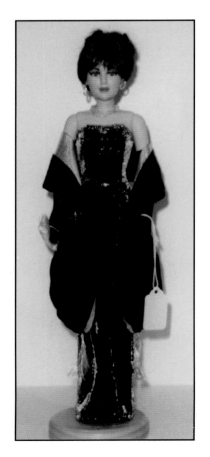

Three of the separately sold outfits that will be available in 2000 for *Eve*. *Photo courtesy of the Susan Wakeen Doll Company.*

Left: Kingstate's *Micki* is yet another new fashion doll for 2000. *Photo courtesy of Kingstate.*

Opposite Page: The most unusual *Barbie*® doll to date, this *Fashion Model* is made of a new material, is strung and has different proportions then traditional *Barbie*® dolls. *Photo courtesy Mattel.*

Delphine Barbie® doll, wearing a diaphanous delphinium blue gown, is the dressed doll offering in the spectacular *Fashion Model* series in 2000. *Photo courtesy of Mattel.*

Chapter Eight

Practically Speaking

In previous chapters, we looked at the hobby of collecting fashion dolls. We discussed the history of our hobby and the dolls that have impacted upon it as well as those that will define it tomorrow. In this chapter, we shift our attention to two important, practical aspects that also impact upon the hobby's health and evolution. First we will look at the Internet, how it has changed the way collectors communicate. Second, we will examine the importance of the secondary market to collectors. Whether or not we enthusiasts are actively involved in buying and selling on the secondary, or non-retail, market, it behooves us all to ensure its health so as to keep the hobby strong and viable into the future.

Without question, the Internet has made a tremendous impact on this hobby, revolutionizing the ways in which collectors communicate, obtain the latest information and buy and sell dolls. The spread of news is instantaneous. Online communities unite collectors literally around the world. Buying and selling can be as simple as the click of a mouse. While many collectors keep up with and enjoy the hobby without having Internet access, it does facilitate and hasten the spread of information and can add a fascinating and fulfilling dimension to the hobby. Moreover, whether collectors are wired to the "net" or not, we all

Dolls outfitted for special events are often desirable by collectors. *Party of the Season Tyler Wentworth*, hair restyled by the author, wears a gown that was limited to 100 pieces, made exclusively for the Nashville Collectors United event 2000, held over St. Patrick's Day weekend.

have benefited because it has helped the hobby develop and grow. For example, *Gene* might not have gained such a loyal following in a relatively short time had it not been for collectors sharing their love and enthusiasm for her via the Internet. In addition, *Tyler Wentworth* and *Daisy* and *Willow* gained a previously unheard of following, inspiring message boards and online clubs months before their release.

Accessible not only via computer but also through the innovative *WebTV,* the Internet has placed at collectors' fingertips a vast array of web sites, electronic bulletin boards and newsgroups, all of which are sources for the latest news and information. Whereas the first *Barbie®* doll collectors gleaned the latest news from newsletters, which were time-consuming (and expensive!) to produce and distribute, today's fashion doll collector can get information instantaneously. Pictures of new doll lines, supplied by the manufacturers or by individuals, appear on the Internet while Toy Fair is in progress, sometimes even before. Special editions can be announced and sold out even before they appear in the pages of magazines or newsletters and the collector who relies solely on print media for his or her news may miss out. However, the emergence of electronic media does not render printed material obsolete as a useful source of information. Although magazines and newsletters are not as immediate as the Internet, they have the advantage of being both permanent and portable. Publications can be set aside for future reference, stored in one's basement or closet for years. Back issues are excellent sources of reference and enjoyment for beginning and veteran collectors alike. In contrast, web sites can be notoriously transient, here today and gone tomorrow. Personal computers can crash, obliterating all one's carefully bookmarked favorite sites in seconds. Moreover, portability will always remain an advantage of print over electronic media. It isn't easy to drag a computer, even a laptop, from one room to the next or to try to use it, say, on a car trip. Because both the Internet and traditional publications have their share of advantages and disadvantages, savvy publications have presence on the "net" as well as on the newsstand to cover the best of both worlds.

Others connected with the fashion doll industry have information-oriented web sites as well. Ashton-Drake, The Franklin Mint, Alexander Doll Company, L. L. Knickerbocker Company, Susan Wakeen and Robert Tonner all have web sites that list and occasionally market their wares. A trend for the future may be the proliferation of personal web sites set up by the designers themselves. For example, Doug James and Laura Meisner are currently working on a site on which they will offer tips on tweaking *Daisy* and *Willow* in order to display them at their best as well as tidbits on 1960s fashion styles. In addition, many doll shops are online. These retailers are excellent and expeditious sources of news that has been passed to them directly by the manufacturers themselves. Retailers on the "net" are poised to meet the needs of those consumers who want to order around the clock and not wait for regular business hours.

Individuals not affiliated with publications or manufacturers also disseminate information on the Internet. Personal web sites and home pages offer literally everything from histories of the various dolls to light-hearted pictures of dolls posed in amusing scenarios. There are sites that offer the latest "hot gossip" as well as some that provide hints for display and customization. Other sites promote individual artisans who create and sell handcrafted furniture, doll stands, clothing and accessories for the various dolls as well as those who provide services such as rerooting, repainting and other forms of doll customization. There are even sites that promote other sites. The brainchild of collector Jerry Parzer, *Blossoms Awesome Links* (http://www.blossoms.net) is one of the most comprehensive, providing links to a staggering number of various sites.

For the most part, the companies and the designers of the dolls are pleased that enthusiastic individuals care enough to include information and pictures of their dolls on personal web sites. However, the web site owner needs to include a disclaimer that he or she is not affiliated with the company or individuals whose dolls are pictured or discussed on the site. The prudent collector may also wish to inform the company that he or she is setting up a web site to commemorate that company's dolls. In addition, the web site owner should use his or her own images. Permission must be obtained before using images that appear in magazines, catalogs or other web sites. "Borrowing" an unauthorized picture from another source without crediting or informing that source is a violation of copyright law and can have serious consequences.

In addition to web sites, another source of information on the Internet is the electronic bulletin board. Major providers, such as *America Online (AOL)*, often maintain message boards on which members can post on related subjects. Internet mailing lists, such as *egroups*, are similar to bulletin boards except that the posts are sent directly to each subscriber, individually or in a digest. Online clubs like those sponsored by *Yahoo!* also maintain message boards upon which the members can post. Some of these clubs and mailing lists are moderated, which means that while freedom of expression is permitted and encouraged, there are guidelines that may prohibit the use of profanity or regulate the number and frequency of buy/sell ads. Generally, one must

Lani was a limited edition *American Model* created by the Robert Tonner Doll Company for the 1998 Collectors' United Gathering. She is the first *Model* to sport this face mold with this particular skin color.

register for membership and often that membership must be approved by the board or list moderator. Some are open by invitation only or have waiting lists. The message boards on *AOL* are similarly moderated, but are open to any *AOL* member.

Not only do the electronic bulletin boards and online clubs provide for the sharing of information, they also promote a sense of camaraderie among the participants. Many "newbies" report that they often felt alone and isolated before discovering the existence of the "boards." Questions are answered, discussions are inaugurated and information and enthusiasm are spread among the members. Participants share their triumphs, personal as well as those associated with the hobby, and many find the "boards" to be a safe haven in which to commiserate or just ask for emotional support. Many lists or clubs organize holiday swaps, online "conventions" or other cyber-events that further contribute to a sense of community. Some online groups organize charity drives of donations of money or items that benefit those in need. Among the most innovative ways of raising money for charity online is having individuals contribute their talents or goodies for a customized doll that is later auctioned off, with the proceeds benefiting various worthy causes. In a day in which people are often too busy to attend club meetings or even keep up with pen pals, online camaraderie can be a viable and welcome alternative.

While the Internet can certainly enhance the collecting experience, one must be aware that it has its drawbacks. Sometimes the race to be the first with the news leads to the spread of misinformation as hastily posted information may be inaccurate or incomplete. Honest mistakes can be taken as the gospel truth. Rumors run rampant and are often embellished or convoluted as they circulate. Statements may be taken out of context and opinion and speculation can be misconstrued as actual fact. Even when information is posted accurately on one board or web site, it can be misinterpreted when passed along.

Another disadvantage to the Internet is the anonymity. It can be intimidating, if not downright frightening, to deal with strangers on the Internet, especially in any transactions that involve money. Online auction services like *eBay*™ have safeguards that permit buyer and seller to check each other out. One can look at someone's feedback to determine if he or she has had problems completing transactions in the past. However, nothing is foolproof and fraud can and does occur on the "net." Although most people who buy and sell on the Internet are honest, the collector must exercise caution and prepare to take action should a transaction go sour.

The anonymity of the Internet can also lead to a breakdown in civility. Online fights can erupt easily, escalating into vicious "flame wars" that can polarize the virtual communities built up around clubs, lists or boards. "Flaming," which is posting something that attacks or insults another person, is the online counterpart to making an obscene hand gesture to another motorist. Just as an obscene hand gesture can generate road rage, so too can "flaming" bring about Internet rage. Surely, Internet rage, while not physically lethal the way road rage can be, is dangerous nonetheless. It tears apart friendships, renders safe havens unsafe and destroys the trust and camaraderie of a public board. Indeed, it makes a mockery of the sensibilities not only of those involved in the "flame war" but also of innocent bystanders.

Each individual who participates in a public message board or online club or has a web site should be aware of proper "netiquette," the application of both good manners and common sense that one would utilize in any other social situation. For example, one should not state something in an e-mail or in a post that one would not say to another person face-to-face. Additionally, while controversial opinions are welcomed and often lead to fascinating, thought-provoking discussions, those opinions should be expressed with respect, not with the intention of putting down another person or collectible. Frankly, there is no reason for name-calling or scathing comments made in the pretense of wit and humor. Someone can respectfully state why he or she does not care for a particular doll without viciously attacking that doll, the people behind it and the people who love it. Every doll (not to mention every collectible!) is someone's favorite. Before you publicly denounce a doll as "ugly" or worse, think about how you might feel if someone posted something similar about your favorite. This is not an encroachment on freedom of expression. Serious issues, negative aspects of collecting and problems need to be addressed in order to be remedied. Disagreements happen. However, there is a difference between freedom of expression and sheer nastiness, and in order to make the "net" enjoyable for everyone, the most basic principles of etiquette and respect must be kept in mind.

Yet another drawback is that the instantaneous nature of the Internet has led to an expectation for immediate gratification. We can get our news immediately; why can't we get our dolls immediately as well? The result is that waiting can

Opposite Page: *Fortune Teller Cissy* was a special edition created by the Alexander Doll Company for the 1999 Collectors' United Gathering. She is the first *Cissy* to be made with this particular skin color.

Meet Me in Paris Gene was a special edition created for the Paris Fashion Doll Festival 2000. *Photo courtesy of Vince Nowell.*

become intolerable and patience can wear thin. An illustrative example is the situation with *Tyler Wentworth*. When pictures of the doll surfaced on the Internet even prior to her debut at Toy Fair 1999, collectors became inordinately excited. Anticipation built up rapidly and was so intense that many collectors felt bitter frustration when the dolls, already scheduled for release late in the year, were delayed even longer. In contrast, had collectors not learned of *Tyler* until her debut in a magazine, weeks or even months after Toy Fair, the wait between her introduction and distribution would not have been so long. We collectors need to keep in mind that while communications have sped up via the "net," not everything else in life has kept pace.

Another area that has been greatly impacted by the Internet is the collector's secondary market. The advent of online classifieds and Internet auction services like *eBay*™ has completely changed the channel that collectors use to buy, sell and trade. Why travel to a distant doll show or wait for magazine classifieds when one can buy or sell much more easily on *eBay*™? Moreover the immediacy and convenience of Internet transactions has affected the secondary market as well. There are many more players, buyers and sellers alike, on the Internet secondary market and, as a result, that market has become extremely volatile. Rapid and extreme fluctuations in supply and demand can make prices vary wildly in very short periods of time. Something can sell for a certain price and a week later, sell for significantly higher or lower, depending on the precarious balance of supply and demand.

A healthy secondary market is essential for the hobby's long-term survival. Keep in mind that not every collector has gotten in "on the ground floor" with every doll. Some who are new to the hobby or to a particular doll may be content with purchasing current market dolls, but others will want to backtrack and amass some or all of the earlier editions they missed. In addition, not even the most devoted collector can attend every event or acquire every exclusive edition. The secondary market thus provides a means for collectors to find convention dolls or other special editions, a far better alternative to missing out altogether.

Another reason the hobby needs a healthy secondary market is to provide collectors with an avenue for selling unwanted or excess dolls. Every collection grows and changes, lest it becomes stagnant. Similarly, collectors' tastes evolve over time and the doll that was a must-have yesterday might become tomorrow's biggest regret. The need for money or space can also motivate a collector to sell. While indeed most of us collect for enjoyment, not for profit, it behooves us all to ensure that secondary market prices remain healthy and stable. It is demoralizing and devastating to put a significant amount of money into a collection and then have to sell it for a fraction of its retail price. Thus, a balance must be kept between supply and demand by fashion doll manufacturers, merchants and collectors ensuring that both buyers and sellers are satisfied.

One way to keep the secondary market viable is through responsible speculation. While speculation on a grand scale, such as what happened in the contemporary *Barbie*® market, can wreak havoc, conservative speculation ensures that there will be a supply to meet the demand, whether immediate or long-term. Keep in mind that prudent speculation does not mean hoarding, nor does it mean snatching up everything available then trying to sell it to fellow collectors who missed out because you were there first. There is a difference between the sort of moderate speculation that nurtures the hobby and the speculation fueled by sheer greed, that hurts the hobby by creating a false demand, leading to an oversupply on a saturated secondary market.

No one has a crystal ball that can predict what might be in demand in the future. Especially with this genre being so young and the market so mercurial, it is imprudent to try to second-guess what might be "hot or not" tomorrow. However, there are common-sense guidelines that the collector can keep in mind that can optimize one's potential return as well as preserve the integrity of the secondary market.

1) For the most part, the smaller the edition number, the greater its desirability on the secondary market. This is especially true in cases in which the edition is a small fraction of what is normally in the line, say, an outfit limited to 100 when most are limited to 2500.

2) Is the item a "first?" Often the first year's line is more desirable on the secondary market than items from subsequent issues. An item that is first of its kind, such as the first convention package or the first exclusive created for a shop or event may also be more in demand in the future.

3) Is the doll aesthetically pleasing to most collectors? If it's unattractive, poorly conceived or of inferior quality, the secondary market demand might not be as great as it would be for a beautiful piece of obviously high quality. And quite frankly, if you don't like something, why spend money on it? Chances are that others may not care for it either and you may be stuck with it for a long time.

4) If you choose to speculate on collectibles still available from merchants, pay no more than the suggested retail. It makes no sense to buy something for future resale at an inflated secondary market price when the market can change rapidly. There is no guarantee that you will be able to sell an item for what it cost you, especially if you bought it at a higher secondary market price to begin with.

5) Prepare to wait a while before your item increases in desirability. It's unrealistic to buy something and expect to sell it almost immediately for any sort of profit. Most things must pass the test of time in order to become desirable on the secondary market. However, there are exceptions to this, such as convention dolls or packages that are more in demand immediately after the event or items that are withdrawn quickly from the market.

6) Unless you are forced to sell out of financial need or for other reasons, don't sell your items for less than their original retail price. Doing so, while a boon to collectors seeking bargains, creates an impression that something is less than desirable or not worth the original price. Moreover, when one seller begins "dumping," others panic and follow suit. The supply is increased although demand has remained constant, and, as a result, secondary

Tyler Wentworth's first event exclusive was the *Market Week* fashion, sold to attendees at a gala fashion show presenting the 2000 line the night before Toy Fair.

market prices tumble. Savvy buyers seeing such a trend wait for prices to drop even further, decreasing demand, and that downward spiral leads to a weakened market.

7)   When speculation is no longer enjoyable and becomes an obsession, stop. Nothing kills the joy of collecting more efficiently than becoming obsessed with making money off one's collectibles. Concern with turning a profit can make the acquisition of new dolls burdensome rather than pleasurable. When you consistently see dollar signs instead of dolls, quit.

Naturally, most of us collect because we love our dolls, not because we intend to cash in quickly and earn huge profits. However, in order to keep the hobby vital and alive, we collectors must ensure the survival and health of our secondary market. It is possible to speculate without being greedy, and prudent speculation can be a very enjoyable aspect of the hobby. The secondary market must be approached with respect and fairness in order to achieve a balance that is beneficial to the hobby and all collectors concerned, buyers and sellers alike.

What will be the "hot" doll of 2000? Many collectors eagerly look forward to Susan Wakeen's *Eve*. *Photo courtesy of the Susan Wakeen Doll Company.*

Opposite Page: This version of the Franklin Mint's *Jackie Doll* was created in a strictly limited edition of only 25 for the 1999 Doll and Teddy Bear Expo East. *Jackie* is dressed in a pink suit worn by the First Lady on Valentine's Day after her husband's inauguration. The stand and certificate of authenticity were hand-signed by Oleg Cassini. *Photo courtesy of The Franklin Mint.*

This *Miss St. John Cissy** was rewigged and dressed in the outfit from the 1996 *Onyx and Lace Cissy*. Rewigged by author.

Chapter Nine

Your Collection Your Way

The new generation of fashion dolls has literally changed the face of the hobby, attracting scores of enthusiasts who never would have imagined themselves as doll collectors. Before I became interested in fashion dolls, I never would have dreamed that someday I would be an avid doll collector—and, chances are, most readers feel the very same way. So why do we collect? How do we collect? How do we decide between all these wonderful dolls that are available? And how can we optimize our enjoyment while, at the same time, promoting the hobby and inviting others to join in our fun?

For every collector, there is a different reason why he or she collects fashion dolls. Frankly, to cover all these reasons I would need a few extra chapters! However, we can draw a few conclusions and succinctly sum up a few of the motivations fashion doll collectors have in common.

First, we have a passion for fashion, even though it is not necessarily a part of our everyday lives. Society and its accompanying rules of style have changed dramatically over the years. Whereas fashion was once extremely rigid, today anything goes. In many instances, "Casual Friday" has taken over the entire workweek. At home, we savor our comfort, lounging around in jeans, sweatshirts and sneakers. How many of us would really trade our favorite duds for tightly corseted waists, treacherously high heels and white gloves worn all day, every day? And even if we didn't mind suffering for style, where on earth would we wear such garments? To the grocery store? To pick the kids up at day care? I don't think so. Through our dolls, we can indulge our passion without pain or impracticality. We can visit different eras in fashion, experiment with styles that would not suit us in real life and flit back and forth between vintage and contemporary. We may live in jeans and *Birkenstocks* but we are fashionistas by proxy, courtesy of our dolls.

Second, our fashion dolls reflect us. They are our three-dimensional mirrors, our vinyl counterparts, embodiments of our most cherished dreams. They represent our younger selves, our idealized selves and our inner selves. We look through our dolls' wardrobes and are flooded with memories of what we wore, what our parents wore, what our children wear today. And how many of us have looked into the face of a doll and seen someone we know? Maybe we've even seen ourselves.

Moreover, our dolls embody our fantasies. We can play out being Hollywood stars, Mod birds in swinging London, Seventh Avenue sensations, or, as Glenn Mandeville has written, beautiful girls with beautiful lives. Indeed, we can even fantasize about being of a different gender, age or ethnic background through our fashion dolls. And we can succinctly express those facets of ourselves that are perhaps incongruent to our real lives. We can enjoy *Alex's* navel-baring ensemble without scandalizing the local PTA. We are complicated, interesting people and, in turn, our collections are complicated and interesting as well.

Third, our fashion dolls enhance our creativity. Mandeville has also written on several occasions that we can drape our dreams on our dolls. Isn't that eloquent? We drape our dreams on our dolls. Indeed, we sew for them, we repaint their features, we re-root their hair or change their wigs and we make jewelry and accessories for them.[2] It's just like when we were kids, cutting our *Barbie*® dolls' hair or fashioning crude outfits out of rickrack and felt—only now we know what we are doing! Indeed, it is amazing to go to a doll convention or check out the offerings on web sites and *eBay*™ to see the explosion in the trend toward customizing fashion dolls. Some collectors keep their work and others sell or give it away. Regardless, it is creativity in action, inspired by our dolls! Furthermore, while this trend may be relatively new to doll collecting, it has been happening for years with other hobbies. Customizing action figures is literally an art form for many enthusiasts, and there is a massive proliferation of fan fiction based on popular TV shows, Japanese animation and "sci-fi" series. It's time fashion doll collectors caught up!

The seemingly endless number of choices facing the collector of contemporary fashion dolls can leave one's head spinning. How can you decide what to get and what not to get? Perhaps the best—and only—guideline is to follow your heart. This is, after all, YOUR collection and you need to satisfy only yourself, no one else. You best know your tastes and preferences. Yes, there can be peer pressure in collecting. It's hard to admit you don't care for a doll that enthralls everyone you know. Likewise, it's hard to stand up for a doll that you love when no one seems to share your feelings. However, you don't have to follow the crowd. It can be exhilarating to get caught up in the latest

---

Notation: All customized dolls, those that have been altered by private individuals not associated with the manufacture of these dolls, are denoted with an asterisk (*). Please note that they are, for the most part, one of a kind and are NOT available from retailers.

2 Any changes to the doll that cannot be completely reversed will not be as desirable to collectors and therefore its value may be adversely affected.

collecting craze, but it's empty and meaningless (not to mention costly!) if the current rage doesn't speak to your heart. Listen to yourself, to what you are saying inside. If you don't want a certain doll, don't buy it and don't be pressured into adding it to your collection.

However, do keep your heart open to new experiences. Collectors sometimes cheat themselves when they don't want to try something new. "I like what I collect and I don't want anything else," can be a logical, legitimate statement. Or it could be an excuse to stay stuck in a rut. In your heart, you know which it is. And please don't mistake others' enthusiasm for peer pressure. If a friend gushes, "You have to get this doll," he or she may only be trying to share the fun. Relish your friends' passions and remember that you can appreciate something without having to possess it.

Don't be hard on yourself if you make mistakes. Beginners and veterans alike all make mistakes. We pay too much and we sell for too little. We regret buying this and not buying that. Don't gnash your teeth and let a mistake ruin your enjoyment of the hobby. You can minimize your mistakes, of course, by being knowledgeable and well informed. But don't agonize. Don't flagellate yourself over a missed opportunity or a doll you probably should not have purchased. It's not worth the angst. The hobby is meant to be fun.

Also, don't become obsessed with numbers. What might be too many for one collector is too few for another. Each of us has his or her own comfort point, that level of saturation at which we are satisfied. If we have too many dolls, we want to dispose of some. If we don't have enough, we buy more. Again, don't try to keep pace with your collector friends, for each of us is different. It isn't the number of dolls you have that makes a collection special; it's the number of dolls that are special to you that makes the collection!

There is one thing, though, that I urge every fashion doll enthusiast to do. Please play with your dolls. Play is such a wonderful, essential part of adult life but is all too often overlooked in the face of deadlines, housework and the other chores of daily life. We sit in front of our televisions and watch other people play; instead, we should be bringing that play into our own lives. And what better tool than our fashion dolls?

Remember, our fashion dolls are meant to be handled. They are not purely ornamental and intended to be stashed away in curios or behind glass. Ornamental dolls undoubtedly have their fans as well as their special niche in the hobby. However, one would never dream of dressing a Lisa Lichtenfels soft sculpture beauty or repainting an exquisite wax doll from the team of Paul Crees and Peter Coe. These dolls, truly unique works of art, are meant to be left as is and admired.

But with unbreakable, mass-marketed contemporary fashion dolls, the sky is the limit!

Play can provide a respite from adult life. The ubiquitous television blurts out news of children shooting children, women marrying millionaire strangers and politicians tearing at their rivals' throats. I suppose psychologists would say that by playing with our dolls, we are nurturing our inner children. I prefer to think that we are just getting back to a simpler time in life and reliving tactile memories of play. Moreover, the creative manipulation of a doll can be comforting and an ideal way to relieve tension. Look at how comforting hobbies such as needlework or knitting can be. It's no different with our fashion dolls. Playing with a doll can give you a break, just a few minutes away from the stresses of daily life. I am not advocating sticking one's head in the sand, playing with dolls to the point of becoming oblivious to reality. However, just a few minutes of play every few days can be mentally healthy and fortify our spirits so we can face the challenges in the world. Adult life is hard and at times it can be depressing and demoralizing. Everyone needs some sort of respite. When we look at the ways in which people try to cope with stress, falling into addictions to everything from food to mind-altering drugs to self-destructive behavior, isn't playing with dolls a much saner alternative?

Play can be as simple or complex as you would like. It can be simply turning a doll's head or lifting her arm, redressing her or combing her hair. It can be as complicated as doing a total makeover, repainting, rerooting or rewigging, creating our own outfits or accessories. We might choose to position our dolls in interesting ways, say, sitting on a shelf, surrounded by other collectibles or we might enjoy creating elaborate dioramas, seeking out just the perfect miniatures and creating our own little capsules that catch time and hold it still.

Whatever we do to play, we are infusing our dolls with our personality and our dreams. Sometimes dolls speak to us exactly the way they are. Personally, I would never dream of altering my beloved *Iced Coffee* or *USO Gene* dolls because they so succinctly speak to my heart that there is no way I could make them reflect my dreams any more. This is a wonderful communication between designer and collector, two disparate hearts sharing a similar vision. However, we also have freedom. We can accept or reject the original premise of a doll, her story, her wardrobe and even her name. We can view that doll as a blank slate, a canvas on which we can bring our fantasies to fruition. Our dolls travel through time, hopping from one era to the next, sometimes sharing each other's wardrobes. Some collectors change their dolls' names. My friend Linda Braun

704
PATTERN/PATRON
ONE SIZE
UNE SEULE TAILLE

0704 / O/S

0 31664 31026

vogue® craft

Gene™

© 1999 Mel Odom. Represented by Bliss House, Inc. West Springfield, MA 01009-4123

Above: Realizing the importance of "hair play" for adult collectors, Ashton-Drake introduced in 1999 *Simply Gene*, a basic doll dressed in a swimsuit, with bendable legs and long hair that could be styled. Instructions for different hairstyles were included with each doll. This blonde *Simply Gene* has had her hair cut and curled. She is wearing the beloved ensemble *Goodbye New York*.

enjoys renaming her *Cissys* to reflect what she sees as unique in each one; one doll is dubbed "Crystal" for her beautiful blue eyes and another is "Autumn" to commemorate the time of year in which she joined Linda's collection. Ultimately, the choice is ours. We can infuse our dolls completely with our own personalities or we can intertwine our visions with those of the original designers. As long as we are enjoying our collection, the possibilities are endless.

In her essay *Twelve Dancing Barbies*®, published in the book *The Barbie*® *Chronicles*, famed author Erica Jong writes, "The truth is we need *Barbie*® dolls for grown-ups, too. All our lives would be enriched by having a fantasy doll we could strip naked and dress in our dreams." My

word, she's got it! That is a perfect description of the dolls we collect, *Gene*, *Tyler*, the new incarnation of *Barbie*®, revitalized and revamped for the adult enthusiast. The fantasy dolls for which Ms. Jong yearns already exist in the guise of the next generation of contemporary, collectable fashion dolls. From *Alex* to *Willow*, our fashion dolls enhance and enrich our lives. They open the door to our dreams and present us with unimaginable opportunities. They provide a bridge to friends literally all over the world, people with whom we would never have come in contact in our everyday routines. We have magic on our shelves, in our curios and in our hands. It is up to us to keep that magic alive for ourselves and for other collectors, present and future.

Opposite Page and Right: Play is an important part of the *Somers & Field* line, for many ensembles can be worn in different ways. In these two photos, both dolls are wearing the *New Year's Eve* ensemble. However, prototype *Willow* is wearing the optional sheer overdress while prototype *Daisy* is shown without the overdress. *Photos by Steven Mays, courtesy of L.L. Knickerbocker.*

Tyler* undergoes a subtle transformation when rerooted with thicker, darker hair and given a side part. Reroot by author. Outfit by Mari DeWitt.

Right: Collector Randy Wilson created this *Gene** to "dye" for. Yes, it was a process that took months, but he created his own African-American fashion doll by actually dyeing *Gene*.
Photo courtesy of Randy Wilson.

Many collectors enjoy switching their fashion dolls' wardrobes. Here, *Brenda Starr* shines in *Gene's Sparkling Seduction Gown*.

The talented Tom Courtney customized this Tonner *Madeline* into Queen Elizabeth. *Photo courtesy of Tom Courtney.*

Affectionately known in the doll world as the "Number One Tonner Cheerleader," Tom Courtney customized this exquisite *American Model. Photo courtesy of Tom Courtney.*

Sherry Miller repainted this breathtakingly beautiful *Tyler Wentworth**. *Photo courtesy of Sherry Miller.*

Mary Beyer created the beautiful ensemble worn by this rewigged *Daisy Resort Cissy**. Rewigging by author, *Beanie Baby* pit bull terrier by the Ty Company.

Olivia*, an *American Model,* has been completely rerooted and her hair has been braided with over 150 tiny braids. Done by author in her "spare" time.

Mary Beyer painted the face and Debra Aguila-Weinstein of Fabulous Frocks created the gown of this lovely customized *Gene* who now resides with collector Cindy Kent. *Photo courtesy of Cindy Kent.*

References

Bates, Sabrina, "Fashion Dolls." *Doll Reader,* October 1994

BillyBoy*, *Barbie® Her Life & Times,* Crown Publishers, Inc., 1987

Caviale, Karen, "How to Collect *Barbie,* Part One." *Barbie® Bazaar,* May/June 1995

Caviale, Karen, "Mel Odom." *Barbie® Bazaar,* March/April 1989

Cook, Carolyn B., *Gene,* Hobby House Press, 1998

Fecher, Louise, "A Sense of Style." *Dolls,* July 1994

Fennick, Janine, *The Collectible Barbie® Doll, an Illustrated Guide to Her Dreamy World,* Courage Books, 1996

Finnegan, Stephanie, "Extra! Extra! Heavenly Headliner." *Dolls,* November 1999

Finnegan, Stephanie, Sargent, Lia, and Pfeiffer, Walter, *Madame Alexander Dolls, An American Legend*, Portfolio Press, 1999

Graff, Mary, "All About Eve." *Doll Reader*, March/April 2000

Goldstein, Lewis, "An Interview with Robert Tonner." *Doll Reader,* May 1992

Houston-Montgomery, Beauregard, *Designer Fashion Dolls*, Hobby House Press, 1999

Houston-Montgomery, Beauregard, "Gene." *Doll Reader,* August 1995

Houston-Montgomery, Beauregard, "Madame Alexander's Jacqueline." *Doll Reader,* March/April 1997

Houston-Montgomery, Beauregard, "Madame Alexander's New Cissy." *Doll Reader,* September 1996

Henry, Pat, "The Mysteries of Mdvanii." *The FashionDoll Scene,* June 1999

Izen, Judith, *Collector's Guide to Ideal Dolls, Second Edition,* Collector Books, 1999

James, Sallie, "A Preview of Robert Tonner's 1993 Dolls." *Contemporary Doll Magazine,* April 1993

Jeffords, Barbara, "*Barbie Bazaar* Celebrates 10 Years." *Barbie® Bazaar,* July/August 1998

Jong, Erica, "Twelve Dancing Barbies." In *The Barbie® Chronicles: "A Living Doll Turns Forty,"* ed. McDonough, Yona Zeldis, Touchstone, 1999

Judd, Polly & Pam, *Glamour Dolls of the 1950s &1960s, Revised Edition,* Hobby House Press, 1993

Judd, Polly & Pam, *Hard Plastic Dolls, 3rd Revised Edition,* Hobby House Press, 1993

Judd, Polly & Pam, *Hard Plastic Dolls, II,* Hobby House Press, 1994

King, Constance, "Madame La Parisienne." *Doll Reader,* September 1999

Mandeville, A. Glenn, "A Star is Born!" *Doll Reader,* September 1999

Mandeville, A. Glenn, *Contemporary Doll Stars,* Hobby House Press, 1992

Mandeville, A. Glenn, *Doll Fashion Anthology & Price Guide, 6th Edition,* Hobby House Press, 1998

Mandeville, A. Glenn, "How to Collect *Barbie.*" *Barbie® Bazaar* Special Edition, 1996

Mandeville, A. Glenn, "Meet the Mod British Birds!" *Doll Reader,* July 1999

Mandeville, A. Glenn, "Taking Stock of *Barbie* Dolls." *Barbie® Bazaar,* May/June 1996

Mandeville, A. Glenn, *The Golden Age of Collectible Dolls 1946-1965,* Hobby House Press, 1989

Mandeville, A. Glenn, "The History of *Barbie* Doll Collecting." *Barbie® Bazaar,* July/August 1998

Mandeville, A. Glenn, "The History of the 1950's Fashion Doll," *Barbie® Bazaar,* March/April 1989

Mandeville, A. Glenn, "The Many Faces of *Barbie,* Part Four." *Barbie® Bazaar,* July/August 1995

Mandeville, A. Glenn, "Toy Fair 1996." *Barbie® Bazaar,* May/June 1996

Mandeville, A. Glenn, "What is a Fashion Doll?" *White's Guide to Collecting Figures,* August 1999

Meisner, Laura, "Gene Marshall." *Barbie® Bazaar,* January/February 1996

Meisner, Laura, with James, Doug, "Somers & Field." *Miller'$ Fashion Doll,* August/September 1998

Menchine, Ron, "Move Over *Barbie,* Here Comes *Gene.*" *White's Guide to Collecting Figures,* July 1996

Mixon, Doris, "BillyBoy* Alive and Well." *Miller'$ Fashion Doll,* August/September 1999

Nestoras, Bessie, "*Cissy* on 7th." *Dolls,* March/April 1999

Noble, John Darcy, "*Gene*—A New Star Is Born." *Contemporary Doll Collector,* October/November 1995

Noble, John Darcy, "Rare and Scandalous." *Doll Reader,* December 1995/January 1996

Pursley, Joan M., "Changing Times at the Alexander Doll Company." *Dolls,* November 1990

Richter, Lydia, and Joachim F., *Collecting Antique Dolls,* Hobby House Press, 1991

Sabulis, Cindy, and Weglewski, Susan, *Collector's Guide to Tammy,* Collector Books, 1997

Sanders, Jill, "Elegant Perfection: The Dolls of Robert Tonner." *Contemporary Doll Collector,* November 1999

Starner, Teri, and Lewis, Janet, "*Barbie's* Turning 40: Where is the Market Heading?" *Barbie® Bazaar,* January/February 1999

Stitsworth, Adele, "*Ginny,* The Fashion Leader in Doll Society." *Miller'$ Fashion Doll,* October/November 1998

The Editors of *Doll Reader* (Cook, Carolyn, Kinsey, Michilinda, and Wood, Scott), *I Had That Doll!* Park Lane Press, 1996

Tosa, Marco, *Barbie® Four Decades of Fashion, Fantasy, and Fun,* Harry N. Abrams, Inc., 1998

Wantanabe, Sumiko, "Deux-L and *Barbie*." *Barbie® Bazaar,* September/October 1989

Wantanabe, Sumiko, "Dheei, the Ultra Neo-Zéphyr of Black Fashion Dolls." *Barbie® Bazaar,* May/June 1992

Wantanabe, Sumiko, "Mdvanii, the Renaissance of Fashion Dolls" *Barbie® Bazaar,* November/December 1990

Wilson, Jacqueline, "Madame Alexander's *Cissy*." *National Doll World,* March/April 1989

Advertisements:
FAO Schwarz Exclusive Cissy: Dolls, November 1990

Lady Luminous: Barbie® Bazaar January/ February 1990, November/December 1990 and March/April 1993

Mdvanii: Barbie® Bazaar January/February 1990, September/October 1991 and March/April 1993

Tonner: *Barbie® Bazaar* March/April 1993 and September/October 1994

Catalogs:
Alexander Doll Company 1952—1961, 1993—2000

Effanbee 2000

Family Company 2000

Robert Tonner Doll Company 1988—2000

About the Author

Beth Owens is a freelance writer and avid fashion doll collector. For five years, she was a regular, prolific contributor to the various *Miller'$* publications, including *Miller'$ Fashion Doll* and *Miller'$ Market Report*, for which she wrote the popular *Pink Prerogative* column.

A former registered nurse, Beth is married to Dr. David Owens and has two sons, Charles and Andrew. She is also "mother" to two cats, Oliver and Madeline, and a female crayfish named Bob.

Index